Judge* Hoff, Jesus Loves You but the Rest of Us Think You're an A**hole!

Tales from my 20 years as a
San Francisco Court Commissioner

by Agatha Hoff

ROBE
WARRIOR
PRESS

San Francisco • California

Designed by
A Book in the Hand
San Francisco, California

Cover type by
Grace Ann Jensen

ROBE
WARRIOR
PRESS

To contact Agatha Hoff,
email agathahoff@gmail.com
or go to www.agathahoff.com.

Dedication

To Zelma Russell, Jane Wallet, Julio Howay, David Lee,
Lloyd Hill, Gene Reed, Lesley Sadhu, Anamaria Birdsong and all
the other courtroom clerks, police officers and bailiffs —
survivors all — who suffered with me through the years and
without whose help I would have cried instead of laughed.

And to court commissioners everywhere who do whatever judges
don't like to do and manage to laugh at themselves now and then.

Foreword

Introduction

Approach the Bench

This Man Died and Left No Forward 15

It's the Last Door on the Right 19

The Hall 23

On the Blink 27

With My Eyes Closed 31

Bumps on the Road to the Bench 35

To This Day, They Tell the Story in Des Moines 39

Dancing at The Hall 43

A Pig in a Poke 47

The Iguana was Driving 51

A Bike Named Charlie 55

Ever Wonder What the Judge is Thinking? 61

The Armpit of the Law

In and About Old City Hall 6 7

Love and Lust in Family Court 7 1

Christmas Visitation 7 7

Disaster Preparedness 8 1

Not Exactly Sugarplums 8 3

The Armpit of the Law 8 7

For Whom Pro Bono Tolls 9 1

A Child is Born 9 5

Through the Looking Glass 9 9

Sunrise in San Francisco 1 0 3

Eureka 1 0 7

Confessions of a Court Commissioner

Roaches, Roaches Everywhere 1 1 3

I Dreamed I Kissed your Hand, Madame 1 1 9

The Truth or Not the Truth 1 2 3

Convent Girls in The Closet 1 2 7

Stars Above the Naked City 1 3 1

The Little Redheaded Boy 1 3 7

The Ghost Rider 1 4 1

My Mongolian Ancestors 1 4 3

Is the Grass Greener? 1 4 7

Tourists: You've Got to Love 'Em 1 5 1

Confessions of a Court Commissioner 1 5 5

Look Ma, You're Flying 1 5 9

Home Is 1 6 5

Acknowledgments

FOREWORD

I love Agatha Hoff's new book, *Judge* Hoff, Jesus Loves You, but the Rest of Us Think You're an A▪hole!* Her wise and witty reflections perfectly capture the daily drama that plays out before the trial court, from heart-breaking child custody fights to preposterous visitation wars over one family's pet pig and everything else in between. One memorable passage is like a snapshot of a judge's afternoon calendar and contains a list of what caused the day's relationship to end: "He loved the bird more than he loved me." "She brought home the 16th cat." "The soup was too hot." "He threw out her teeth." "She routinely beat him up." As judges often note, you can't make up the stuff that happens in court.

Only a traffic commissioner would know that many people refer to their cars by name. We're not talking "Toyota" here. We're talking "Peola." One can vividly imagine the shaken parents from Ohio who visit their son in his Castro Street job, pick up a ticket for failing to curb their wheels, and later muse in court, "I just wish we knew whether it was us or your city that had our boy turn out the way he did." And my favorite: the scofflaw who went through a flashing red light, arguing his innocence because, "I went through on the blink."

As Hoff observes, "People revealed bits and pieces of their lives, that were only remotely connected to the court appearance." In these vignettes, rich with detail, dialogue, and humor, the reader is treated to an insider's view of the justice system. What our insider reveals are sad, touching, funny, and true tales, told by someone with a big heart and a huge commitment to justice.

— Lynn Duryee, *Judge, Marin County Superior Court*
Author of *Hooked on Drug Court* and *Trial & Error*

* *Let me be perfectly clear: I was never a judge!*

INTRODUCTION

When I was a little kid, I loved parades. It became clear to me on the very first day of my assignment to preside as a court commisioner, that I had landed a job as the grand marshal of an endless parade of the human race.

Having scribbled bits and pieces about life for years, I immediately realized that I had a goldmine of stories on my hands. From the very first litigant who appeared before me in traffic court, wearing a T-shirt emblazoned with the words "Fuck You," to the next, who apologized for the first man's apparel, I jotted down notes. And as the years passed, small claims court and family court became part of my world.

Humanity with all its foibles showed me glimpses of lives lived. Often poignant, truths or half-truths or outright lies during testimony were expressed in ways that tickled my funny bone and made others in the courtroom laugh out loud.

As I developed my notes into stories, it occurred to me that events in my own life provided the same mix of humor and pathos. I threw a few of those tales into the mix, so those who read this can laugh at, as well as with me.

Agatha Hoff
San Francisco Superior Court Commissioner (Ret.)

Approach
the
Bench

In traffic court, the foibles of the human race, with all its prejudices, pathos and humor, were always evident in a day's mail. I have included excerpts from the many memorable letters I received while presiding in traffic court.

"I will have an operation on my butt. Approximately a quarter of my butt will be removed. I will definitely be disabled for four or five months. Unable to sit in a chair, let alone walk any distance. I need mercy or a new court date. God bless."

THIS MAN DIED AND LEFT NO FORWARD

In 1981, when I heard the title of my new job with the San Francisco court — "traffic referee" — I visualized standing by a parking meter while a meter maid and motorist slugged it out over the hood of a car. When the parking meter emitted a clang, like the bell at a prizefight, I imagined bringing down a flag in resolution of their dispute. Years later, the title changed to commissioner, and my prizefight image dimmed.

I dispensed justice in traffic court for 13 years. Day after day, hundreds of people came during morning and afternoon sessions for "Instant Hearing — Parking Ticket Protest." As though on a hiccupping conveyor, each person told his or her story, stayed only for seconds, received my verdict, and then faded away.

Every morning, my clerk placed a file folder requiring my attention on my desk. The file was inscribed with the title, "Parking Correspondence" and contained the incoming mail from the previous day. These letters were my reward at the end of my day in court when time had at last stemmed the tide of humanity passing before my bench. Now I could sit back in my chambers and read. In the letters, I received glimpses of people's lives, sometimes funny, sometimes poignant, depicting their struggles coping with our rapidly spinning world.

Opening the folder, I would begin to dispense justice-by-mail. One letter, written on stationery bearing a heart-shaped logo displaying the faces of five children of multiethnic backgrounds, was an objection to a ticket for a missing license plate:

> "With regard to the enclosed ticket, I urge you to consider this issue. I am a social worker employed at the Tenderlion Childcare Center. While at work, one of my disturbed patients removed my front license plate, which bears my name "Felice," in order to have a part of me. I have recovered the plate and screwed it back on my bumper."

What a wonderful transposition of the "loin" into a "lion" for a childcare center located in the tough Tenderloin neighborhood of San Francisco. My correspondent had no doubt met many a tender lion in her work. When I read the letter I had a vision of some poor lost soul sleeping with Felice's license plate.

Often, I received mail from visitors to the city from rural areas. This one arrived from Cazadero, north of San Francisco, near the Russian River:

> "Hello:
>
> I know you've got a lot to do, but please relax and read:
>
> Inclosed is the two tickets I got by parking in your city overnight: THIRTY DOLLARS!
>
> San Francisco and my cabin in the woods are two different worlds. I am a simple man, I harvest the trees in my garden, carry my water and chop wood for my home. Last year I made an average of eighty-seven dollars a month in honest work, for I take no food stamps or unemployment, etc. etc, — I pay my way in this world. I trade for many of my needs, grow a few things but use a little money for food (four to six dollars for weekly groceries).
>
> My point is city people use more money, have more than I, so its value is less — you are in the main flow of it.

I ask that justice be tempered with mercy. Utilize the heart in this case. This is society, humanity in action — please can we waive this (to me) exorbitant charge for standing still on a residential street?

This lesson has not gone unlearned; I will use great care when visiting the city, if again I borrow a car to visit my loved one.

Please recognize my situation and act as appropriate with your feelings.

Thank you for your attention. Peace in your heart."

I never knew which of these letters were real, and which had been written by an imaginative motorist. At times, I gave the authors Brownie points for sheer poetry, particularly when the return address was from a sufficiently remote location, that would have meant coming to court to dispute the ticket in person would have cost the driver more than the fine involved.

Often, the protesting writer referred to his vehicle by name. Frequently, the tickets had been issued to some other vehicle. If the person entering the citation into the court's computer had made a mistake, the computer would generate a notice to the wrong car owner:

"Dear Sir:

Enclosed you will find a copy of a parking ticket for my Toyota pick-up truck named Peola! She is a grand and gallant lady that does not leave the Marysville and Sacramento area. She is along in years, and her giddy-up is not what it used to be. For her, to visit San Francisco is prohibited strictly by her family, and she understands.

January 1st, we purchased Peola from my daughter. "I need more reliable transportation," said Laura loudly! She and I agreed, and the pickup is now "retired" and goes only to Lindhurst High

School and back. I am a teacher and Peola and I are both slowing a bit. On June 2 (date of violation), she (Peola) was resting on the school faculty parking lot. My 148,000-mile truck has never been to San Francisco.

I know you will find the mistake and let us know as soon as possible.

Please! Please! Don't say we made a mistake — we did not!!!

Thank you and have a nice forever and do without my twenty-three dollars. Love from both of us.

P.S. What the hell are you doing to us?"

Perhaps the ultimate in protest came written across the face of a demand for payment of a parking ticket, which had been issued to a Mr. Sander. In a shaky hand, Mrs. Sander had written:

"This man died and left no forward."

IT'S THE LAST DOOR ON THE RIGHT

The cockroach turned his vulnerable belly toward heaven, wiggled his legs in a last attempt to right itself, and gave up the ghost. I sighed as I observed the roach on the linoleum floor of the ladies' room. The start of another routine Monday, at the Hall of Justice in San Francisco.

The other court commissioners, who act as judges in the various courts, often complained because the court did not provide restrooms in our chambers. However, I considered using the public facilities as a sort of fringe benefit. The judges of the Superior Court, who had their own toilets, really didn't know what they were missing by not having had the opportunity to observe the daily goings-on, or to read the graffiti, which often eloquently described them on the restroom walls. My own ego was kept in check by a daily review of the opinions of those who passed before me. Here's my all-time favorite:

"Judge Hoff, Jesus Loves You, but the Rest of Us Think You're an Asshole!"

Some of the great issues of the day played themselves out in that dismal bathroom. I remember the royal debate that raged over whether George, a probation officer who was undergoing a sex change and who had not yet had his penis removed, should be allowed to use the women's bathroom. Memos flew back and forth between various court administrators. This was a problem without precedent and had no easy solution. It puzzled me as to why anyone who still had the proper appendage to sidle up to a urinal would want to stand in line with the women, but there is no accounting for human desires. Eventually, the offending member was removed, and peace once again descended on the ladies' bathroom.

The volume of traffic in the restroom increased as the weekend neared, matching the increase of business the previous night in the red-light district of San Francisco.

When I entered the ladies' room one Friday morning, after what must have been a busy night in the Tenderloin, a sea of pale skin that seldom saw the light of day, fishnet stockings, tank tops and bleached hair confronted me.

I had a hard time getting near the sinks to rinse out my coffee mug. They were all in use by ladies of the night who had just been released from jail and were bathing. Over the months of my tenure in traffic court, I had come to be on a first-name basis with a number of regulars. Gloria, Alice and Jasmine, who staked out the three washbasins that morning, tended to be arrested every month or so and had spent the night in the sheriff's hotel.

Jasmine was fair-haired, much prettier than the other women. She had very blue eyes, a wide, smiling mouth and smooth, long hair the color of straw.

Gloria, like many of the girls, wore heavy pancake makeup, blue eye shadow and glossy lipstick to camouflage the ravages inflicted by her profession.

Alice appeared to be the oldest of the three, her face wrinkled by years of smoking. She stubbed out a cigarette in the sink just as I pushed open the bathroom door. That Alice was stripped naked to the waist no longer shocked me the way it had the first time I encountered this scene. Her oversized purse lay open on the floor, skimpy lace bra protruding, douche bag and foil condom packets clearly visible.

I reached in front of Alice to wash my coffee mug, while she scrubbed away last night's makeup with a paper towel.

"I hear Georgette's become permanent," Alice remarked to no one in particular, referring to Georgette's completion of her sex change.

"Yeah," Gloria replied, "I even helped her with her makeup the other morning. She looks damn good."

"Pass me my lipstick, will you, Habitat?" Alice requested, nodding toward her purse. It took me a second to realize that she was addressing me by the name emblazoned on my mug, which read "Habitat for Humanity." I chuckled and complied with her request.

Georgette had had to adjust to so many changes. George ate cheeseburgers and milkshakes! However, recently I had observed Georgette nibbling on salad and sipping a diet Coke in the cafeteria. I'd overheard her complain while eating lunch that the same salesman who had tried to sell George a car by highlighting various features under the hood, now was focusing exclusively on the vehicle's color scheme, when trying to conclude the sale.

The cockroach remained belly up on the bathroom floor for several days. It belonged to a long line of pedigreed roaches, which I had routinely disposed of over the years. Fumigation or some other drastic measure had never been employed.

On Wednesday, I encountered Jim, the janitor, wearing his blue wrap-around apron and deferential smile. His English skills had been exhausted by our exchanged "good morning"s. He nodded vigorously when I led him to the bathroom and pointed out the dead roach. He smiled. Unable to identify the language Jim spoke, my end of the conversation was similarly handicapped.

The next morning, I drew a circle around the cockroach with a red marking pen, to give Jim a further hint that it needed to be removed, but nothing happened.

After a week had passed, I decided it was time for action. As children, my friends and I had enjoyed staging elaborate sendoffs for various insects, and I thought a similar event would add levity to life at the Hall of Justice. I posted a notice with a big red arrow pointing at the remains:

"Funeral for Cuca to be held at high noon Friday. Mourners to bring candles and join the procession. All are welcome."

I prepared a matchbox, lined with a napkin from the basement cafeteria, and awaited Friday. I envisioned prostitutes, commissioners and assorted criminals being followed by our smiling janitor, bearing the casket to cockroach heaven. I had every intention of going through with the ceremony. Alas, it was not to be. On Thursday, a zealous public defender posted a formal notice on the restroom wall, calling a halt to the proceedings:

1. When a death occurs, the County Coroner must be notified within 12 hours.

2. A determination must be made whether the deceased died of natural causes.

3. A proper death certificate must be obtained before burial can take place.

By afternoon, both the funeral notice and the warnings from the public defender had been translated by an unknown benefactor into five languages and duly posted above Cuca's body.

Friday morning, the light in the bathroom was burned out. Someone had propped an old tennis shoe in the doorway to enable us to see. There was just enough light to discern that one of the translations must have hit its mark, because the corpse and all the notices had disappeared.

A shaft of light from the hallway illuminated the newly scrawled graffiti above the spot where the corpse had been. It read: "R.I.P. Cuca." I couldn't help but smile as I removed the shoe to let the door close behind me.

THE HALL

For those who work in civil court, going to the San Francisco Hall of Justice, where criminal cases are handled, may seem to be the equivalent of slumming. Some who work there develop a perverse love for the place. There is something about that massive gray stone building, with its cavernous lobby, that has crept deep inside my bones. Perhaps it is the never-ending parade of society flowing through the criminal courts building that warms one's soul.

On any given day, the Hall is mostly populated by those who have performed the jaywalking ballet, crossing the four lanes of traffic on Bryant Street. The public defenders (P.D.s) have their offices on Seventh Street, forcing them to make this suicide dive. Crossing at the corner of Seventh and Bryant would add at least 10 feet to the distance between their offices and their destination. Assorted clients tag along behind the P.D.s, with the tacit understanding not to make eye contact with the cops who are jaywalking in the opposite direction, headed for coffee at the deli across the street from the Hall.

More crooks assemble at the Hall of Justice at any given time than anywhere else in San Francisco. As if there weren't enough of them there on their own steam, the sheriff's non-stop express delivers busloads from the San Bruno County Jail to the basement elevators. Metal doors can be heard clanging as these prisoners are dispersed throughout the building. The sound could be coming from the jail on the sixth floor. The rear elevators that disgorge prisoners to the hallway separating the judges' chambers from the courtrooms have steel accordion gates. They sound like cage doors locking. Or perhaps the sound comes from a holding cell door, where the defendants are waiting for their court appearances.

In spite of all the gates and locks, one day some years ago, someone managed to clean out all the wallets from the judges' jackets. The jackets had been hanging on the inside of their chambers' doors while Their Honors, dressed in robes, presided in the courtrooms across the corridor. The place is crawling with cops and sheriff's deputies, but anything not nailed down can walk off. Sometimes, even things that are nailed down or screwed in can disappear. I lost two side-view mirrors from my Toyota, parked in direct view of the police dispatchers. That was in the good old days when judges and commissioners were provided so-called secure parking places in the lot where the new jail now stands. I shudder to think how the judges' cars now fare, since they have been relegated to a lot out of sight of anyone, around the corner of the building, under the freeway.

I like the fact that, with the possible exception of some up-and-coming deputy district attorneys and a few high-priced defense counsel, very few elitist lawyers do business at the Hall. Perhaps the more modest demeanor is the humbling effect of cases lost and lives altered. The ghosts loiter in these hallways.

There seems to be an unwritten dress code among lawyers who practice criminal law, again with the exception of young district attorneys (D.A.s): suits are to be somewhat rumpled, nondescript gray or tan, seldom cleaned. Bottom-of-the-barrel defense counsel add a bulging, tan leather briefcase, well-worn at the corners, to their costume. Public defenders carry stacks of files, too big for briefcases. As for the D.A.s, the uniform consists of navy blue suits with sincere white shirts and conservative ties. They, too, stagger under the weight of stacks of file folders.

Past the metal detectors, in the lobby of the Hall, only a pane of glass separates the hunters from their prey. Southern Police Station is located just inside the front door on the west side of the building. Seasoned, corpulent veteran sergeants mix with newly minted eager beavers just released from the Police Academy. Most cops regard those passing on the far side of the glass with an air of practiced disdain.

The names of police officers killed in the line of duty are chiseled on the east wall, a stark reminder of the seriousness of the business conducted in this building.

The sheriff's deputies, who inhabit the second and third floors, where the criminal courts are located, contrast with the police. They are cast more in the role of zookeepers than guardians of order. It's their job to control the chaos and keep the wheels of justice turning as smoothly and safely as is humanly possible.

On Mondays, when the fresh pool is assembled for the week, wide-eyed jurors roam the building, seeking the jury assembly room. Some clutch their purses protectively to their bosoms, along with summonses calling them to civic duty. Some are eager to serve, others rehearse sob-stories on each other, which they want to try out on the judge, in an attempt to get themselves excused.

An army of civil servants provides the grease for the mill of justice. They move through the masses of people in the corridors, never making eye contact, praying that no one will stop them to ask for directions. They hope to reach the inner sanctum of their offices or courtrooms, undisturbed.

Judges and commissioners inhabit the back stairs, locked-off corridors, chambers and courtrooms, rarely mixing with those who appear before them. I found, though, that I could come and go at will in the public areas, unrecognized and thus unaccosted, simply by donning my bicycle helmet. It would instantly brand me as part of the army of messengers who dash in and out of the building and are generally ignored.

Some hapless Vehicle Code violators, heading for traffic court, join the crush of defendants and lawyers waiting for elevators. The looks on their faces reveal their feeling of superiority to those headed for criminal court. They are here to debate the principle of the thing. The fact that retention of their driver's license may depend on the outcome of their hearing is incidental to their mission.

A galaxy of prostitutes mixes with other miscreants outside the misdemeanor courts. Some lean against the wall with the bemused expression of those who've traveled this road before.

When the building is locked for the night and only the occasional click of handcuffs and cops' voices from Southern Station disturb the uneasy quiet, a legion of mop-and-bucket-toting Latino janitors appears, and soon salsa music drifts from behind closed doors. These workers will render the Hall of Justice habitable in short order, so that the wheels of justice can grind again in the morning.

ON THE BLINK

Little did I know that the ticket issued to my car when I parked at a broken meter would lead to a career. Years ago, my first experience with traffic court occurred when I decided to protest that citation.

On the day scheduled for my appearance, an obviously senile gentleman presided in a tiny, stuffy courtroom tucked away between the banks of elevators and the public restrooms on the second floor of the Hall of Justice.

Within minutes of the start of the court session, it became evident that the police officer assigned to provide security in traffic court was standing behind the judge not to save him from harm, but to whisper recommended decisions into the venerable gentleman's ear. The judge would then regurgitate what he heard the officer say to the defendant standing before him.

Thus my broken-meter citation vanished into oblivion when His Honor pronounced sentence as "suspected," having misheard the officer's admonition to "suspend it." My next encounter with His Honor took place at a Queen's Bench function, where he amiably chatted total nonsense with female members of the association devoted to furthering the progress of women in the legal profession. To top off the evening, on being introduced to an attorney whose name was Mary, the judge started singing, "Mary had a little lamb."

As a result, I wasn't surprised a few days later when an ad, posted by the

Municipal Court, appeared in The Recorder, seeking applications for the position of traffic referee. The judge's days presiding in traffic court had obviously come to an end.

When interviewed for the position, I assured the panel of judges that the large volume of dissolution cases I'd handled at mass hearings while employed by San Francisco Neighborhood Legal Assistance Foundation qualified me to fairly and expeditiously dispose of the procession surging through traffic court.

Any dreams of glory I may have envisioned associated with becoming a bench officer were soon dissipated. The Clerk of the Municipal Court caught up with me outside the door leading to my chambers as I arrived for work on my first day as a traffic referee. He administered the oath of office in front of the jail elevator just as it was disgorging a load of prisoners clad in orange jump suits on their way to arraignment courts.

I mounted the bench anticipating the first session of the day. The very first litigant who strutted up to the podium in front of me continued to hold my ego in check. He was wearing a white undershirt emblazoned with "Fuck You" in black lettering. The first decision of my judicial career was to tell Mr. Motorist that freedom of speech had its limits. If he wished me to hear his case, he needed to take himself out of the courtroom, proceed to the men's room down the hall, turn his T-shirt inside out, and return.

Soon I learned that all varieties of folks, from all walks of life, turn up in traffic court: teens sprouting orange mohawks, backpackers toting their worldly possessions, UPS drivers, cabbies, unemployed actors (many auditioning their parts as famous defendant wanna-bes) and joggers decked out in their running outfits who seemed to pause at the defendant's podium as though jogging in place at a red traffic light.

At every session, there would also be those (mostly the elderly) who dressed in their Sunday best and acted with dignity and decorum. My first day was no exception. The graying gentleman who followed the T-shirt-clad sloganeer to the podium said, "Your Honor, I apologize for the conduct of that man," as though somehow he had been personally responsible for the other man's rudeness. He then launched into his own story about the invisible fire hydrant that had caused his car to be cited.

Though all testify under oath, the elasticity of the truth and the creativity of litigants can be quite astounding:

"The arrows on the No Parking sign seemed to point to the other side of the street."

"I don't live near where the ticket happened."

"It's not my car — belongs to my friend Adolfo."

"I left my blinkers on, so the battery ran down, so they cited me for a loading zone."

Perhaps my all-time favorite came in protest of a ticket issued to a defendant who had run a flashing red light without stopping:

"But Your Honor, I went through on the blink."

All my pillows still have the tags on them,
so this letter tweaked my attention:

"Since I am one of those people who
never tears the tags off my pillows
because of the warning of federal
offense, you can believe me when
I say I am compulsive about my
obligations. However, I found myself
feeling this violation was unfair. The
more I thought about it, the more
unfair it became."

WITH MY EYES CLOSED

As a court commissioner, my assignments were sometimes at the Hall of Justice and other times at City Hall. Keith McHenry was the link between the two locales. A burly, freckle-faced, red-headed Irishman, Keith came to traffic court at the Hall of Justice on frequent occasions. He usually came to protest a fistful of tickets, many issued to him for parking across the street from City Hall.

Keith and his rag-tag army of helpers constituted an organization called Food Not Bombs. They ran an informal kitchen, serving all comers at Civic Center Plaza. Tickets were often issued because McHenry parked his truck on the sidewalk while he unloaded his folding table and the buckets of soup that he served.

Keith McHenry objected to being cited on the grounds that his vehicle was singled out. Cars driven by law enforcement officers were routinely parked on the plaza, next to his truck. The drivers ran errands at City Hall and were not ticketed. McHenry claimed he was being harassed for feeding the homeless.

On my frequent trips to City Hall, it was difficult to ignore the police and sheriff's department vehicles illegally parked. They lent credibility to McHenry's defense. However, an unrelated case had gone up on appeal from my court. The Court of Appeal, in its infinite wisdom, opined that I was never to use personal knowledge of the location of a traffic infraction when making decisions in traffic court.

I had trouble balancing this opinion with the fact that when I was hired as traffic commissioner, one of the job requirements was a familiarity with San Francisco streets. After the appellate opinion came down, I made every effort to drive around town with my eyes closed.

Since no one appeared to represent The People in traffic court, the cases against Keith McHenry consisted only of the citations issued by S.F.P.D. police officers. No deputy D.A. appeared to counter McHenry's defense of unequal enforcement of the law. Mr. McHenry would generally prevail, and I suspended his citations.

Keith fought running battles against the city on many fronts, but his experiences in other courts and at administrative hearings, dealing with the subject of operating a kitchen without proper permits, were not often successful. As a result, Keith McHenry developed a certain fondness for me and my rulings. I must confess that I felt admiration for his cause. There seemed to me to be something fundamentally decent about taking soup and bread and dispensing it to the hungry, permits or no permits.

Then one particular winter, the heat was turned up on Keith. Once again, the mayor decided to rid Civic Center Plaza of the encampment of undesirable persons living there. The theory was that if McHenry didn't feed them, the homeless would evaporate.

One afternoon on a visit to City Hall, I wore a pale-gray silk suit and a blue-green blouse acquired from Encore, a second-hand store in Marin, which featured discards worthy of royalty. The suit matched my hair and the shirt, my eyes.

As I climbed the open-air stairs from the underground garage to the plaza, I could hear a man yelling through a bullhorn, extolling animal rights. At the stair landing, I felt something hit my shoulder. When I glanced down, the remnants of a rotten tomato were dribbling down the front of my new suit. Apparently some protesters, unhappy with a recent court decision, were lobbing tomatoes into the stairwell. I dug through my purse, found a crumpled Kleenex and wiped the gooey mess off as best I could.

Having learned my lesson, the next time I took the elevator to Civic Center Plaza. As I emerged into a bleak winter afternoon, I noted the usual San Francisco street theater in progress. A group of men huddled around a trash can fire near the elevators as the wind whipped McDonald's containers and paper napkins across the plaza. The Women in Black group, promoting Jewish and Palestinian cooperation stood ignored, at the edge of the park, placards facing City Hall. Keith McHenry's army of Food Not Bombs people had their buckets set up opposite the mayor's office window, dispensing cups of hot soup to bike messengers. Bikes and shoulder bags lay on the dry grass while their owners ate. Disheveled folk lined up, waiting for their turn to be served.

From the garage elevators I cut diagonally across the plaza and walked toward the front entrance of City Hall. On glancing up at the mayor's office windows, I noticed that a camera had been installed on the railing of the balcony. It appeared to be filming the action in the plaza in a continuous sweeping arc.

As I approached the Food Not Bombs installation, Keith McHenry happened to look over in my direction. When he spotted me, he made a dramatic leap toward me and enveloped me in a big bear hug.

"Hello, Agatha!" he cried out. "Smile for the D.A." He jerked his head in the direction of the camera, laughing.

"Wonder what they'll make of my fraternizing with the enemy when they review their film," he chuckled as he let go of me. I could just see some poor deputy D.A. trying to figure out what possible connection I, a court commissioner, might have to Keith McHenry, the bane of his life.

I couldn't resist waving at the camera as Keith wished me an enjoyable afternoon.

Sometimes it was difficult not to hold the sentiments expressed against the writer:

"To Whom It May Unconcern:

I dislike coming to your rat nest of a city as it is, but when you do not even show respect of the proper license, etc. It makes a person wonder what is important in the Gay White Way."

BUMPS ON THE ROAD TO THE BENCH

Fourteen jobs, college, law school and a marriage or two have passed since I worked there, yet the other day I picked up the phone and announced, "Peiser, Cartano, Botzer & Chapman."

"I must have the wrong number," my friend at the other end of the line stammered.

I recognized Jane's voice and realized that my subconscious had unearthed a salutation that I had not used in decades, since my college days in Seattle. This slip of the tongue started me thinking about those long-ago days when I first became a legal secretary.

Peiser, Cartano, Botzer & Chapman (I'd always wanted to add, "Donner & Blitzen," just to see if anyone would notice) was my second exposure to the legal profession.

Back in the sands of time, before women's lib, I worked part-time for Mr. George, a sole practitioner in Seattle, who happened to be very involved in Democratic politics. I would not only bring the usual coffee to him and his clients when requested, but would run out and buy a 2-pound box of Almond Roca candy when his most lucrative clients had an appointment to see him. In election years since, I haven't been able to look at a political ad or a box of Almond Roca without remembering that campaign.

The University of Washington football coach was running for Lieutenant Governor of the State of Washington. Mr. George took it for granted that Coach would be elected due to name recognition. As a result, Mr. George had the unenviable job of grooming Coach to preside over the Senate following the election.

Coach happened to be a rather corpulent, dumb jock (if you'll pardon the expression), so cramming parliamentary law into his brain proved difficult. The candidate would appear promptly at 1 p.m. Monday, Wednesday and Friday afternoons, and sit in an unused office with the day's lesson before him. At 3 p.m., I'd quiz Coach, to see if he had absorbed the assignment. If he regurgitated the material, I rewarded him with two pieces of Almond Roca, his favorite candy. If, as more often was the case, he flubbed the answers, I'd make him wait until 5 p.m. for his next try for the gold-wrapped nuggets. As Coach's hunger increased in the late afternoon, so did his thirst for knowledge, until at last he'd recite the rules on filibuster, or whatever the lesson of the day happened to be, and gobble down his allotment of candy. Around the office we derisively called him, "Mr. Roca."

As predicted, Coach was elected by an overwhelming majority. The man-on-the-street exit poll interviews confirmed that he had been broadly recognized: "Ain't he the coach at U.W.?" they'd say. That, to most people, seemed as good a reason to vote for Mr. Roca as any. He went on to serve for eight years and could often be seen in news clips munching Almond Rocas during debates.

I, an innocent, convent-educated, naive girl of 19, learned about more than politics on that particular job. My reverence for the Catholic Church got a bit of a jolt as well. Mr. George's biggest client was the Archdiocese of Seattle. Nowadays, we no longer blink an eye at scandals involving clerics. Back in the '50s, however, it shocked me that a big part of representing the Archdiocese required my boss to sort through, and at all costs hush up and settle, the sordid lives of clerics of all ranks. Many a lass traveled to Reno, Nevada, all expenses paid, to deliver her baby and give him up for adoption, while the not-so-good Father (father) continued with his priestly duties.

Besides taking care of the archbishop's pressing problems, Mr. George had a general practice, now a rarity among city lawyers, but a common way of doing business in those days. He represented whomever came through the door of his somewhat Rumpolish office, well lined with musty books and desks cluttered with files. Among other things, Mr. George did a smattering of immigration law. Thanks to that part of his law practice, I learned about the nuances of interpreting.

At the time, strict quotas had been imposed by Congress for entry into the United States. Many Eastern European refugees emigrated to Canada and then tried to sneak across the border. Some chose Seattle as their destination. A few were caught and hauled into federal court. Mr. George took on some of their cases pro bono. Eager to help my former countrymen, I translated for Hungarian border-crossers, both in and out of court.

When the new influx of refugees streamed through the courts, a problem arising from the immigration judges' ignorance soon became apparent. Had they been asked, I doubt if some of them could have located Hungary on a map, and most were unfamiliar with the political situation there. (During my early years in America, when I told people I came from Hungary, they often inquired in what state "back East," Hungary was located.) On the other hand, the Hungarian immigrants who appeared in court were unaware of the prevailing ignorance about their homeland. They trusted the system of justice in what they considered to be the promised land.

In the '50s, the McCarthy era was in full swing, and no judge in his right mind would give asylum to Communists. After the Russian occupation in 1945, though most Hungarians hated the occupiers, it became almost impossible to hold a job without becoming a Communist Party member. People joined the party in order to be able to find work.

At the immigration hearing, when the judge asked, "Have you ever been a member of the Communist Party?" and the refugee answered "Igen" (Yes) and recited his or her explanation about the necessity for party membership, I would translate the answer to what the judge needed to hear, by launching into an account of the horrors of torture and prison that awaited the person, were he or she forced by the court to return to Hungary.

Thirty years later, as a court commissioner, I often heard litigants give long answers in their own language to a question I had posed. The interpreter would respond with a suspiciously condensed version. For a fleeting moment, I would think of the members of the sizable Hungarian community in Seattle who owed their prosperous life in America to creative translation.

My economic circumstances necessitated my becoming a night student and obtaining full-time work as a legal secretary. Peiser, Cartano, Botzer & Chapman was the next stop on my road to legal education. The name partners represented a huge natural gas company and looked down their noses at some of the underling associates who earned their bread and butter by taking personal injury or dissolution cases. It added comic relief for me to visualize them all as Santa's reindeer.

It shouldn't have surprised me, therefore, that Rudolph appeared one day, bulbous red nose and all. Mr. Scott, the husband of one of the lesser clients, showed up rip-roaring drunk during the lunch hour, when I was alone in the office, manning reception. He brandished a gun in my face, demanding to see his wife's attorney.

"I'm going to evis- eviscer- eviscerate the bassard," he blurted, waving the revolver in my direction.

"He's out with the flu," I lied, heart pounding, keeping an eye on his trigger finger, ready to duck.

"I shink I'll wait," he said, swaying from side to side. He reached for a chair, stumbled and collapsed in a heap in front of my desk, passing out.

I learned to tread lightly in the lives of divorcing clients.

Many more life experiences would follow, before a fly in a lunch salad would lead me to apply to law school, but that's another story.

TO THIS DAY, THEY TELL THE STORY IN DES MOINES

People often told wonderful stories when they appeared before me in traffic court. One morning, I looked over the sea of faces of those who came for Instant Hearing — Parking Ticket Protest and spotted a pair who subsequently told a pathetic tale. The middle-aged couple nervously held hands. The buxom woman wore a black dress with white polka dots. The man had a ruddy complexion and looked uncomfortable in his suit and tie. They appeared to be tourists, not local miscreants.

To alleviate some of the inevitable boredom of listening to hundreds of traffic stories every day, I liked to try to figure out what some of the defendants were accused of, before they told their tales. I searched through the pile of tickets in front of me and found what I guessed would be the one belonging to the out-of-town pair. Attached to a court slip for an Albert Watson was a citation for parking in a tow-away zone. Sure enough, when I called the name, the couple, still grasping each other's hands, timidly approached the bench. They turned out to be vacationers from Iowa.

Mr. Watson nudged the missus and whispered, "You tell the judge, Mary."

Mary, whose hair was pulled back in a bun, revealing a face gleaming with nervous perspiration, glanced from side to side.

Too much time spent in downtown San Francisco, I thought.

She launched into her story:

"Your Honor," she said, "we were booked into the San Franciscan Hotel at Seventh and Market. Our travel agent in Des Moines told us the location would be OK since we wouldn't be in the hotel much anyway. Well, Judge, it was not OK. Every time we went out the door, we were accosted. When we walked north, there'd be the prostitutes, west the drug dealers, south ..."

"The judge don't want to hear all that, Mary," Mr. Watson interjected.

"Anyway," Mary continued, "we had a miserable first week and, when we complained to the hotel manager, he said, 'I tell you what, I'll cut the rate in half over the weekend. You book yourselves into the Claremont across the bay, leave your gear and the car here and just take BART over and have a good time.'

"So that's what we did. And that sure was a grand place ..."

"Stick to the point, Mary," Mr. Watson again quietly interrupted.

"Anyway," Mary went on, warming to her story, "on Sunday we took BART back, and Judge, you won't believe it, but we were coming up the escalator from the station," and here her brown eyes widened considerably as she continued, "and there were these nuns, but they weren't nuns." She grimaced and screwed up her face as her husband turned beet-red next to her, "and then there were these men on motorcycles but oh, no, Judge, they weren't men ..." and here her eyes opened to their widest, "they called themselves Dykes on Bikes ..."

In the courtroom, tittering became audible. I tried hard not to smile as it became evident that the Watsons of Des Moines had surfaced on Market Street in the middle of the Gay Freedom Day Parade.

I told them that they need not tell me the rest of their story, that their ticket was dismissed.

"You must have parked on the parade route before the tow-away signs for the parade were posted," I told them.

"Why, how did you know, Judge?" Mrs. Watson sounded astonished. "We're going back home today," she added, her voice trailing off.

The relief registered on Mary's face made me smile, and she smiled back.

"We never seen such goings on in Des Moines, Judge," Mr. Watson remarked as he took Mary's hand and led her from the courtroom.

"In November I came back from India and was physically, spiritually and emotionally incapacitated. I moved into a friend's loft because I had no income. I was concerned with graduate school applications, getting a fulltime job, making art, my Jungian therapist, Chinese meditation classes and psychic healings to help me deal with the charred vortex of emotions I had, having just lost my true goddess love.

I write you this to show the human side of my tumultuous personal life and my delinquency. I had not any motorcycle tickets for three years previous to this ticket. Within six months, my life was in shambles. I signed the motorcycle over to a machinist and packed all my possessions and moved to New York, where there's more opportunity and no car hassles."

DANCING AT THE HALL

Often the Hall of Justice bathrooms provided glimpses into the devastating fallout on individual lives created by ongoing trials.

On a dreary winter day, a middle-aged woman stood leaning on one of the sinks, screaming at herself in the mirror.

"Fuck this shit! I ain't gonna die in no cell. Fuck, I's goin' through the change. I's bleedin' to death. Shit, I ain't gonna bleed to death in no cell ..." Her tinted reddish hair, gray roots showing, dangled into her face, covering her eyes as she spoke. My stomach knotted just listening to her.

"Excuse me ma'am," she said, realizing she was no longer alone. "I ain't crazy, I's just upset."

"It's OK," I replied, feeling as if I'd invaded a private conversation. "Take care of yourself and good luck to you."

I followed her out into the corridor and watched as she squared her shoulders, glanced back at me with an enigmatic smile and hobbled into the courtroom across the hall.

* * *

Another morning, I opened the door to the handicapped stall in the bathroom. There, to my horror, lay a young mother, sound asleep with a baby in her arms, their bodies contoured around the toilet bowl. I retreated to the corridor and summoned a female bailiff.

"It happens from time to time, Judge. They stow away for the night from the cold," she explained, as though it were the most logical thing to do. "I'll take care of her."

I paused outside the bathroom door to sort out my feelings. I leaned against the wall for a moment and closed my eyes. The last line from a Sanskrit verse my grandfather had taught me when I was a child came to me unbidden: "I am alone and find my way." I hoped the young mother would.

Their image still haunts me.

           *   *   *

I found that people-watching was at its finest at the Hall early in the morning, before the courtrooms were unlocked for business. I made it a point to walk the block-long hallway from my courtroom to the clerk's office most days before starting work. For a voyeur like me, it was a regular feast to watch as the corridors filled with strutting regulars, anxious first-time offenders and officious bailiffs. Clerks posted computerized printouts of the day's calendars near the courtroom doors. Private counsel riffled through papers. Some of the attorneys appeared to be well-heeled, brimming with self-importance.

When I saw Rosenkranz or Silverstein, two of the more prominent members of the criminal bar, I envisioned them entering Judge Rosten's courtroom. The defendant they represented would be brought there by sheriff's deputies moments later. His handcuffs would be removed, before the bailiff announced the judge's arrival and everyone would stand. Let the show begin, I thought, and wished I could follow the lawyers into court to watch.

Other lawyers in the hallway, wearing ill-fitting brown suits and scuffed shoes, were there to represent low-level miscreants.

Even if I didn't know some of them, I could easily distinguish assistant public defenders from assistant district attorneys in their navy blue suits and white shirts. The P.D.s frequently looked just a bit rumpled. Both the deputy D.A.s and the P.D.s lugged armloads of files, which they tried to balance while selecting the file of a particular litigant or witness.

One morning, on my way to pick up my mail from the clerk's office before the morning court session, a balding Caucasian P.D., with a face resembling lumpy porridge, caught my eye. He was in earnest conversation with a frowning young Hispanic client, whose head was tilted a little to one side.

There was something vaguely familiar about the youth. As I watched, he took one step closer to the attorney, to accommodate his own comfort level. The P.D. took a step back. Each of them unaware of what was going on, they repeated these moves over and over. The attorney seemed flustered as the client gestured with his hands to make his points. I observed them in fascination, reluctant to leave, trying to figure out what was familiar about the young man. It was almost time for court, so I dashed to get the mail.

As I entered the clerk's room, it came to me. The frown on that young man's face and the tilt of his head resembled Chico, a Salvadoran teenager who had stayed at my house for a summer a few years before. Whenever he was puzzled by an English expression, he would tilt his head and scrunch up his forehead. In the few weeks Chico was with us, my entire family fell in love with him. Chico bubbled with life and plans for the future. The day after he returned to San Salvador in September, Chico borrowed a friend's motorcycle, strapped his surfboard and guitar to his back, and headed for the beach. As he was passing through a village, a car ran a stop sign, striking the motorcycle broadside. Chico died instantly.

As I returned to the hallway, I noticed that the public defender and the young client had danced their way to the end of the corridor. Silently, I wished "Chico" good luck and returned to my courtroom.

"All the world's a stage," Shakespeare said. Sometimes I wondered if he had spent time observing the dancing in the corridors of the Old Bailey. One performance or another was on at the Hall of Justice every day.

I think old Will would have enjoyed a dance I observed when the alleged miscreant happened to be a well-endowed, bleached blonde, wearing a skin-tight lavender mini-dress. She had been leaning against the wall in a nonchalant pose, comfortably familiar with the system, not in the least bit worried about her situation. She was being interviewed by a newly hired public defender, who alternately frowned and then glanced at his client with a half-smile, trying to avert his gaze from her ample cleavage. I had heard he was fresh out of law school.

The lady in question was an unusually tall Latina, who towered over her vertically-challenged counsel. When she started to speak, she stepped closer to the young white P.D. He stepped back. As the dance progressed, the lady of the night added body language to the dance, swaying her hips just the slightest bit with every forward step, her hands and arms also entering the conversation. Soon she had the public defender backed up against a courtroom door. He could not retreat any further.

It so happened that their timing was just right. Court was about to be called into session. The bailiff unlocked the door from the inside and shoved it open toward the corridor, thus hurling the unsuspecting P.D. straight into the arms of his client, monumental boobs hanging right in his face.

A PIG IN A POKE

From Cross Timbers, Mo.

Dear Your Honor:

First, I would like to apologize for having to type this letter rather than write by hand, but my arthritis has been acting up some and I can't hardly hold a pen. Our young neighbor down the road always has volunteered to type out this letter as I tell her and besides she'll get credit at the next 4-H meeting.

The reason I'm sending this letter is because of an incident that happened while we were visiting your city about the end of June. My wife, Elviney and me, Elmer Johnson, drove up to your beautiful city because our only son, John, said he thought it was about time we had a visit and besides there was something he wanted to tell us.

Not suspecting anything, we got the neighbors to tend the cattle and feed the chickens and commenced to drive up. That was a very nice, though long trip, as being in the car like that cramped my back something terrible. But I must say, it was a trip well worth making and the farthest I've been from the farm since WWII, but that's another story.

Anyways, we hadn't hardly recovered from the trip when

we saw John (our son) and that shock nearly did us both in. We had always been curious about where he worked, so we thought we'd just go down and surprise him. He was working in one of those bars right off a street named Castro and was dressed like I don't know what. Though the place was dimly lit, as best we could make out, he was wearing eye makeup.

Now Elviney and me was raised to respect the peculiarities of others, but when it is one of your own, well, that's another pig in a poke, let me tell you. Elviney and me tried to reason with him and remind him there were plenty of women back in Cross Timbers, if that was any help, but he said no, thanks just the same.

So, as soon as Elviney could get herself back together, we went back to the car to try to collect what was left of our thoughts, when what do we come back to but a ticket, for parking without turning our wheels in. Now, 18th Street, which is what we were parked on, isn't much of a hill by our standards and I did have the parking brake on, just as a precaution from the days when you used to crank up a car and didn't know if it was going to Hell or Ohio, when that thing got started up, if you'll excuse the expression. And the wheels was turned in a bit, so it would have hit the curb before going too far, if it would have rolled in the first place, being in gear and having the parking brake on and not being on much of a slant anyway.

I was all for trying to find the officer what give us the ticket, to try to explain things, but Elviney said she'd had enough excitement to last a whole life's worth of trips and could we just get back to the Travelodge and pack up and get home before anything else happened.

So right now we're at Elviney's sister's house, as the drive home, on top of everything else, liked to do us both in and that brings me to why I am writing this letter.

Seeing as how I don't think that street we parked on was much of a hill and the car was in gear and the parking brake on, is it necessary we pay this? I would just as soon use the money for Elviney's heart medicine but I won't be able to sleep, knowing my name's on some dang computer, saying I'm a lawbreaker, if I don't pay it.

If you will let us know, we will do our best to abide by what you request, as we are both basically law-abiding people. I'm making a copy of this ticket at our county library and will send the original along with the payment, if that is your decision. I just wish we knew whether it was us or your city that had our boy turn out the way he did.

Truly yours,

Elmer Johnson

"My name is Ernest Moore. I got married four years ago, and Carrie added my name to the pink slip of her car. Carrie left me, for certain reasons I won't go into, and moved to the big city. Ever since, I've been receiving her parking tickets in my mailbox. I leave messages with her brother, her sister and her friends for her to call me, but she doesn't. (I guess she's still mad at me, for reasons I won't go into.) I do not know how to get my name off that pink slip; I do not want to go to Sing Sing if I get pulled over."

I was sipping mushroom
soup during noon recess
while I read and almost choked
when I came to the postscript
Mr. Moore had added:

"P.S. If you catch her, take her to jail and tell her to call me."

THE IGUANA WAS DRIVING

Serving in traffic court was truly educational. People revealed bits and pieces of their lives, that were often only remotely connected to their court appearance.

A defendant once handed me a clipping from the Tampa Tribune:

Two Tampa Police Officers reported that while they were patrolling Florida's busy Highway 19, their attention was drawn to a car moving erratically. As they turned on their flashing lights and pulled alongside, they spotted a three-and-a-half-foot green and orange iguana in the driver's seat.

"It looked like this lizard was driving. He had his claws on top of the steering wheel," the officers related.

The cops called for backup and followed the car for a couple of miles until it pulled over. They found the car's owner, Patrick Ruppell, slouched low in the seat. He was arrested on a drunk driving charge, and the lizard was taken to the SPCA.

The officers reported that the iguana, named Finley, was a pretty good driver.

The litigant who presented me with this tidbit complained about the harshness of the penalty for his own moving violation. He had been cited for having a dummy in the front passenger seat while using the carpool lane.

"At least I don't let her drive," said he.

•   •   •

"One too many rides on the night boat to Albany," declared the next defendant, nodding in the direction of the carpool lane violator exiting the courtroom.

"I'm from New York," he continued by way of explaining the Albany reference, "but now I live in Fruitville — Fourth Avenue near Clement," said he, rolling his eyes toward heaven.

"People call it that, just because one house has an 8-foot wooden screw planted in the front yard, next to a house with a huge statue of a Greek goddess, which in turn is across the street from the Mogen David Temple. But I digress ..." and he launched into a routine parking story.

I checked it out on my way home and sure enough, there between Clement and Geary on Fourth Avenue stood the giant screw, the Greek goddess and the temple. I kid you not.

•   •   •

"This morning I spent half an hour at work, three hours at Social Security, half an hour back at work, half an hour at the bank trying to get some checks, as I've run out. Dashed home for an appointment with the fumigator. We've been having roaches, you see. I got there 10 minutes late, and Rose Exterminator was parked in my driveway. I pulled up and blocked him in, so he wouldn't drive away, thinking I wasn't coming. He asked me to go up the front stairs to let him in so he could gather his chemicals from his truck. I went up, unlocked the door and heard the metermaid's motorcycle. I took the stairs two at a time, tripped and fell on the way down — too late — she's writing me a street cleaning ticket.

"I know I'm not supposed to park on my side of the street, but the exterminator was in the driveway — see, here's their bill."

Did you ever have one of those days?

* * *

"Look, Judge, here's 20, though I could swear that that fire hydrant crept up and planted itself next to my car. I'm not gonna argue that one. But this other one, well, I saw the street cleaner — it was quite a distance down the street. Don't raise your eyebrows, Judge. Yes, I saw it, I ain't gonna lie to you. I was helping a friend move some things and just ran a box into the house. I beat the cleaning machine and moved the car out of the way, but I just didn't beat the vanguard of meter maids that descended like locusts on my hapless Camaro. If you let me go this time, I swear I'll take BART when I come to town."

* * *

Next to approach the podium was a twig of a guy and, working her way forward in the courtroom, was a woman as big as a house. They reminded me of Jack Spratt and wife from the nursery rhyme.

"You'll have to excuse my wife because she's a bit slow. It takes her forever to get ready to go anywhere, do anything. She's getting on in years, you see," Mr. Spratt said as he motioned for the woman to hurry.

Deferring to their ages and demeanor, I decided to settle in and let him have his say. This was, after all, their day in court!

"I'll give you an example — I can clean up the kitchen in 15 minutes. When she does it, first she segregates the garbage. All the wet stuff gets plastic wrapped. The paper napkins go down the chute. Then she takes every single dish and washes it thoroughly before putting it in the dishwasher. Now, if by some evil design, someone else has put something in it already, invariably she will rearrange the contents, so all the dinner plates face south, dessert plates east, and so forth. She then takes the forks and puts them in one compartment of the silverware container, the knives in another, spoons in a third. Heaven help us if someone mixes the cutlery.

"Now, the day we got the ticket, she'd sent me down to back the car out." The wife nodded in agreement.

"Said she'd just put on her shoes and be down in a minute. I should have known she wouldn't leave the house without clean shoelaces."

The Mrs. lifted her foot, showed me her immaculate sneakers, laces gleaming, and beamed at me.

"I'm sitting in the Dodge in the driveway," Mr. Spratt continued, "and this fat arm appears out of nowhere and puts a ticket under the wiper blades for parking on the sidewalk. I hops out of the car to tell the meter maid the wife's on her way, but she roars off in her Cushman before I can catch her. Can you believe it, Judge?"

I believe it, I believe it!

●   ●   ●

A young couple approached to make my day:

"This gal and I stood in line so long, signing up for Instant Hearing," the fellow informs me, "we decided to get hitched. Will you marry us, Judge?"

He turned to the smiling bride and inquired, "By the way honey, what's your name?"

A BIKE NAMED CHARLIE

My bike took up an inordinate amount of space in the rear of the courthouse elevator. My fellow passengers frowned when they saw it. I knew they wished that I had left Charlie outside.

Judges Gebhart and O'Hara, both corpulent in the manner of those who eat too many rubber chicken dinners, stepped into the elevator just before the doors closed. O'Hara gave my yellow bike a judgmental glance. Gebhart took care that the robe he carried over his arm didn't touch my bicycle's wheels. I started to say good morning, but both judges turned their backs, oblivious to my identity, hidden under my helmet. They assumed I was one of the army of messengers who scurried in and out of the building, delivering legal papers to the Clerk's Office. Neither suspected that they were riding in the elevator with "Charlie II," or that I couldn't possibly have left my commute companion tied to some pole in front of the courthouse. Charlie, after all, was not just any old bike.

My sister speaks of loving a freckle-faced, redheaded boy in second grade. When she asks me about my first love, I remark without hesitation that it was Charlie, the yellow bucking bronco two-wheeler, jerry-rigged for me in Switzerland.

After World War II, as an 11-year-old runt of a child, I was sent by my parents from Hungary to stay with a family in the Alps. Homesickness struck me with a vengeance. In an effort to cheer me up, Fatti, the head of the house, built the bike for me from remnants of two-wheelers, which had been ridden over the years by various members of his brood of eight children. I fell in love with every inch of Charlie, beginning with his slightly misshapen front wheel, which lent riding a certain excitement.

Charlie had a mind of his own. I became intimately familiar with every pothole in the village. Whenever I thought I had avoided one, the wobbly motion of the unbalanced front wheel would steer me where I did not intend to go. Oh, how I loved that unsightly machine.

Charlie, alas, met his demise, and I very nearly met mine one morning, when we tried to negotiate a sharp right turn at a good clip, and the bike decided to run headlong into an adjacent wall instead of turning the corner.

The bed of nettles at the base of the wall enhanced my feeling of having landed on the wrong side of the pearly gates. Alas, the frame of my little bronco was bent beyond repair, and Charlie lay where he dumped me, smeared with my blood.

A couple of years later, my family and I emigrated to America. As I grew, I qualified as the hand-me-down queen of the universe, inheriting books, clothes and bikes outgrown by my sister or bought as salvage at garage sales. Though their wheels were true, none of these bikes quite engendered the same deep feelings of affection I had felt for my Swiss steed. I loved these bikes in a more fickle, teenage sort of way.

As an adult, I shared my wheels with my four children. As each in turn grew strong enough to sit unsupported, he or she rode either on a seat behind me or on my handlebars, sometimes one kid in each spot, making us look like a humpbacked camel. I like to think that during these rides my love affair with the bike passed to another generation. Sometimes, even now, when I ride across the Golden Gate Bridge, I hear, echoing through the years, the bloodcurdling shouts of my youngest son yelling, "Faster, Mommy, faster!"

For my 55th birthday, I bought myself a new bike. No hand-me-down, no salvage, no prior owner, brand-spanking new. The chrome and the spokes shimmered and shone on its sleek black frame emblazoned with the words "Hard Rock." I couldn't quite believe that it belonged to me. I was, once again, utterly in love.

At sunrise, the day after I bought it, I opened the garage door and hoisted the bike gently onto the rack on my car, before heading for a trail on the other side of San Francisco Bay. In the thirty seconds that it took while I ran upstairs to get my bike lock, someone swiped my prized possession. After a period of intense mourning, I told myself that this romance was not meant to be, and I went back to riding my previous garage sale acquisition.

The next spring, a whole new world opened up to me. I saw a notice in the *Tubular Times* describing biking tours for women over fifty. I blew a wad and signed up to traverse 250 miles through the Blue Ridge Mountains. WomanTours rented me the sleekest bike I'd ever ridden. It had a cobalt blue frame, light as a feather, made of some wondrous material with a high-tech name. Twenty-one gears, no less, made it slide up mountain roads with the greatest of ease. When I pedaled through the parade grounds of the Virginia Military Institute, 1,200 cadets saluted. I thought theirs was an entirely fitting gesture. That bike and I became rain-soaked; we rolled through surreal fog, puffed our way up a 9-mile grade, and sailed down a glorious 12-mile descent, all the while surrounded by the violet Blue Ridge range.

Our laughter echoed through the mountains as the six of us on the tour acted like kids once again. At one point, while riding through a horse farm, we came upon six mounting platforms. In unison, we dismounted our bikes, jumped up on the platforms, spread our arms over our heads in the form of a V, and took Olympic-gold bows in all directions, hearing the applause of thousands ringing in our ears.

At the end of the journey, I could not part with that wonderful bike and, on an impulse, bought it to ship home. When the bicycle arrived in San Francisco, my son Roy, then 33, who used to urge me to go faster, helped uncrate and reassemble it.

Lo and behold, during my first ride through the neighborhood, a garage sale beckoned. I stopped and there, propped against the wall, stood the grownup version of my Swiss bike of long ago. It had that unmistakable bent front wheel of Charlie's. I chuckled as I remounted my sleek Trek 7500.

At the next intersection, a four-way stop, I paused as cars coming from the other three directions pulled to a stop. As I glanced at each driver in turn to make sure he or she saw me before riding into the intersection, I noted the nightmare of all nightmares for a biker. I was surrounded by drivers with cell phones glued to their ears, oblivious to traffic around them and most certainly unaware of me. Hapless souls going through life wrapped in technology. They may never know the feeling of the wind in their face or hear the whir of pedals beneath their feet. I yielded to them all before gingerly riding through the intersection.

I pedaled over to evening services at St. Jude's. (The church is named after the patron saint of lost causes.) I wound my Kryptonite lock through the front and back wheels, and locked the bike to a telephone pole in the alley behind the church. During the service, I prayed to have car phones banished from the earth and all their owners endowed with 21-speed, all-terrain bicycles like mine. I felt very noble, since the prayer I had uttered was not quite the one I'd had in mind at that stop sign intersection. But alas, I think even St. Jude couldn't help me, since God himself must have gone hi-tech. Who else could the guy next to me be talking to on his cell phone in the middle of the service? Perhaps I could e-mail Him to get His attention. www.god.com? Is Anybody there?

I left church to retrieve my Trek 7500. The shadow of a cyclist pedaling fast fell across my path as a youthful rider rounded the corner of the church. I saw the sun glint off cobalt blue and knew before looking down the now-vacant alley, that my wonderful new bike was gone.

I sighed when I saw the cut cable still wound around the pole and hesitated only a moment in memoriam. Then I walked through the alley as fast as I could in the direction of the garage sale I'd visited that morning. Before I reached my destination, I knew with certainty that "my" bike would still be there. We were meant for each other.

There is a God after all, I thought, as there, leaning on the closed garage door, was that decrepit yellow bike with the slightly askew front wheel. Attached to the bike, waving in the wind, I spotted a glorious sign: "Take me, I'm yours," it read.

I had the wheel trued and a new chain put on. I rode Charlie II the six miles to work from my Richmond District home to the courthouse on Folsom Street in downtown San Francisco for two years before I retired. Judges and commissioners often took to the stairs in the building, to avoid having to re-litigate the cases of fellow elevator passengers who had just appeared before them. I never had that problem when Charlie II was with me.

At the end of a long day of listening to sob stories in traffic court, as I shed my judicial robes in my chambers and was donning my cycling togs for my ride home, I could hear the voice of Jack Rhodes coming through the door that led to the corridor.

"Where'n hell does she expect me to park?" he was saying. "She just doesn't understand, but ..." his voice trailed off as he walked away down the hall.

Jack Rhodes, a habitual double parker, had just left my court, having presented me with his 50th variation on the same theme. He had a large van; it didn't fit in most spaces. He had an emergency delivery to make; he didn't have time to go around the block. On other occasions, I had reduced the fine on some of his citations. This time, though, the citing officer had quoted Mr. Rhodes in the comment section of the ticket: "I'll get it knocked down anyhow." Alas, I had made him pay the full fine.

I sighed, as Jack Rhodes' voice receded. I turned to the mirror which I kept tucked in my bookcase between *Black's Law Dictionary* and my copy of Jack Rhodes' favorite, the Nolo Press book, *How to Fight Your Traffic Ticket*, applied my sunscreen, and cinched the strap on my helmet.

As I wheeled my bike out of the office and headed toward the elevators, I could still hear Rhodes holding forth on his bad fortune. His voice mixed with the sound of elevators pinging to announce their arrival on our floor, doors swishing open and closing, other people talking. The elevator lobby had cleared and momentary quiet descended as I approached to push the *down* button. A set of doors promptly opened to reveal Jack, his face bearing an air of sardonic preoccupation as he reached to pound on the *ground floor* button. I had managed to stop his elevator from descending. I hesitated at the thought of sharing a ride with Rhodes, and the doors began to close.

"Well, ain't you comin'?" Jack demanded. "You stopped the damn elevator."

"Sorry," I told him and wheeled my bike in.

"I come down here for nothin'," Jack informed me as we began our descent. "That bitch don't listen to me."

As I muttered a noncommittal response, I realized that my wraparound sunglasses, helmet and dear old Charlie II were working their magic, providing me anonymity. Jack had no idea who I was.

"Hope your day improves!" I called to Jack as we left the building. I hopped on Charlie and headed down the handicapped ramp leading toward Folsom Street. In the rearview mirror attached to my helmet, I could see Jack Rhodes approaching a van double-parked in front of the courthouse. I heard him curse as he reached for the ticket tucked under the windshield wiper.

Ah, the revolving doors of traffic court, I thought, and whistled, "Auf wiedersehen ... à bientôt ..." as I headed for home.

EVER WONDER WHAT THE JUDGE IS THINKING?

One of the greatest challenges of presiding in court is keeping your mind focused on the proceedings. On occasion, however, some testimony or piece of evidence can set off a chain of thoughts completely unbidden.

One day, I heard a small claims case involving a heated landlord-tenant battle over habitability. The tenant was very agitated, wagging his fingers at his adversary. In the midst of sputtering testimony, with dramatic flourish, he tore open a paper bag he had been holding, revealing a jar full of live roaches he had collected in his apartment. He picked up the jar and slammed it on the bench in front of me.

"I rest my case!" he concluded.

The jar shattered and the roaches scattered in all directions.

As the marauding creatures approached, my thoughts switched to a scene recently described in a Moscow newspaper:

> A lonely pensioner in Kazakhstan sits in his kitchen. He is coaxing his new drinking buddy, a cockroach, to become addicted to vodka. He holds an eyedropper and is dispensing a few drops of the fiery spirits onto the table in front of him. The insect emerges from a hole in the wall to guzzle up the liquor. The old man calls

the roach "Vladimir" after a dear departed friend. Once Vladimir has guzzled up the vodka, he retreats to the window ledge, rolls over onto his back and remains in that position, tenderly watched over by his master.

*   *   *

In a matter of seconds, as though someone had placed the next slide in front of my brain, my mind returned to the courtroom just as the first roach started climbing the sleeve of my robe.

Bedlam ensued as the litigants, my bailiff, my clerk and I all swatted and squashed as many roaches as we could. Eventually, calm returned. For weeks afterward, escapees could be spotted all over the courtroom.

When the case concluded, my clerk approached the bench and whispered that when he heard the jar break and saw the cockroaches scurrying, he was surprised to see a faraway look on my face.

"Aren't you glad they can't put pigs in a jar?" he said, reminding me that we had heard a case the week before in which a landlord objected to a tenant wanting to keep a pig as a pet. The clerk smirked at me and called the next case.

My concentration was shot to smithereens with that remark. Hadn't I, just that morning, read in the *Chronicle* of a Spanish pig that was raised as a dog and had gone into a depression when it was forced to live with other pigs? Do you suppose they tried Prozac?

Since the cases in small claims court would often be just as bizarre as anything I could read about, it was no surprise that, as I forced my mind to concentrate on the next case, here's what I heard:

"He loves the bird more than he loves me, Judge."

"That's not true, Phil, and you know it," the respondent spit out his words at the petitioner.

"Gentlemen," I interjected, "please direct your remarks to me." I flipped through the file and realized we were dealing with a divorce, in effect splitting up the parrot, along with the rest of the community property.

"You should hear him talk to Jezebel, if you don't believe me, Judge. He calls that bird honey, sweetheart and every other term of endearment you can think of. He never calls me anything but 'Andy'! Well, that's not quite true, Judge. Sometimes, he calls me 'murderer' and other nasty names."

"That's because he threatens to fricassee Jezebel."

"Gentlemen," I say, "I take it you are in agreement that the parrot belongs to the petitioner." No one objected. "Now, could we please move on to the disputed items?"

So, the next time you are in court and ingratiatingly ask, "What's your thinking on this, Judge?" Be careful — she might tell you.

The Armpit
of the
Law

"If you object to my objections,
I guess there is nothing I can
do except pay, and curse you
privately. But do you know how
much cat food 25 dollars can buy
and the physical and emotional
penalties of living with hungry
cats? You can contact me on
Lopez Island, Washington, where
I have fled."

IN AND ABOUT OLD CITY HALL

Now that the dome of San Francisco's City Hall is gilded and the dot-commers rent cavernous, tastefully decorated spaces for swank soirées beneath it, I suffer pangs of nostalgia for its more rumpled version of yesteryear.

Before the 1989 earthquake, which rendered the building uninhabitable and brought about extensive renovation, City Hall and its environs were a bit run-down. In those days, I worked in traffic court at the Hall of Justice and was paroled twice weekly to do a stint in small claims court at City Hall.

I'd park my car in the underground garage at Civic Center, across the street from the home of the civil courts, which in those days were located on the third and fourth floors of the building. Not having the patience to wait for elevators, I would climb the stairs from the lower floors of the garage to the plaza above. The smell of urine mixed with Lysol greeted me the minute I cracked open the iron-barred fire door of the garage, leading to the stairwell.

Emerging from the darkness into the sunlit plaza, I'd encounter encampments of the homeless, shopping carts piled high with their belongings hidden under black plastic garbage bags. Sycamore trees stood naked in the winter, the pool around the fountain drained — used once too often by street people as urinals, I suppose. The pool and the fountain have since been bulldozed, replaced by flowerbeds and pristine grass.

Harry, one of the regulars who lived in Civic Center Plaza, invariably approached when he spotted me coming out of the northwest stairwell.

"Can you spare a dollar?"

I'd smile at him but shake my head. He'd then give me an expectant grin and add his trademark phrase: "I'll take American Express."

Nowadays, nobody greets me.

Today the plaza is patrolled, the homeless have been cleared out and have relocated themselves one block east, to United Nations Plaza, out of sight of the mayor's office. In the '80s, members of the Food Not Bombs organization had been ever-present and the Women in Black, held up signs proclaiming their cause: "United Israel and Palestine." I wonder now whether their zeal has survived the current upheaval in the Middle East.

In those days, brigades of men — who in my mind I classified as "gray suits" — looking self-important, carrying shiny briefcases, hurried through the shopping cart brigades, to make their way from the garage elevators toward the entrance to City Hall. Today the "suits" head for the new courthouse across the street, and those entering City Hall are just as likely to be sightseeing tourists, as those doing business there.

On entering City Hall in the good old days — which in some respects I guess weren't so very good — the search for a cup of coffee led me to the belly of the beast. It didn't seem possible, but the cafeteria, back then, managed to be even bleaker than the one at the Hall of Justice. In the basement, graying white bathroom-tiled corridors made me think that a line of urinals would be just around the corner. The tiles wound around, under stairs, in and out of overflowing broom closets with doors ajar.

The smell, not of coffee, nor of dough rising, but of stale cigarettes, enveloped me. As I rounded a corner, smoke billowed out of the open doors of the coffee shop, a free-to-smoke zone by tradition. The first time I saw the smoke, I thought City Hall was on fire. The coffee resembled dishwater.

From the basement to the third floor, where the civil courts were located before the '89 quake, large marble tiles lined the lower half of the walls along the stairs. The day of the quake, some tiles popped off, frightening people trying to flee the building.

The only metal detectors then in evidence were at the family courts. Violence in civil guise at City Hall? Now they are at all entrances of the building.

The courtrooms were wood paneled, with huge windows adding to the grandeur of their appearance. There was no air conditioning at City Hall in pre-quake days, making the courtrooms sleep-inducing for judges, lawyers and litigants alike on warm afternoons. "How To Nap With Eyes Wide Open" should be taught at Judges' College.

I recall a commissioner — who shall remain nameless — from my lawyering days. She routinely stumbled up the steps to the bench to work off her martini lunches. To get air into the courtroom, she would order the bailiff to open the windows. This, however, brought in the sound of the ever-present jackhammers from the street outside, which drowned out the witnesses. The other alternative was to turn on the giant overhead fans, which must have taken up residence on the ceilings sometime in the 19th century. They roared like lions. None of this, however, prevented Her Honor from falling asleep the instant she leaned back in her leather chair.

In late afternoon, when it was time to retrace my steps to leave the building, I would often spot local politicos scheming on the grand staircase connecting the mayor's office to the ground floor, under the rotunda. These impromptu meetings continue to this day, but somehow — under the current remodeled, pristine conditions — they don't seem to have the old scummy flavor.

Jake, another homeless inhabitant of Civic Center Plaza, often reminded me that I had spent my day working the "civil" side of the law. He'd sidle up to me as I left City Hall and inquire: "May I pinch your bottom?"

At the Hall of Justice, nobody asked.

"Sir or Mom: I received this tiket on a
meter #906 which at the time the tiket
was given the meter was in a horisonital
possion, also jamed and would not
opperate. The meter woman had to
almost get on her knees to see if it was
violated. In my oppion she did not show
to much inteligence. I tried a number of
time to call the number on the tiket but
the line was always bussy. I believe this
tiket was verry illeagle because the meter was not in oppoeration at that time.
I must take time off work which cost me
financialy for the lack of inteligece of
one of your employies."

LOVE AND LUST IN FAMILY COURT

When the San Francisco Municipal and Superior Courts merged, I became a Superior Court Commissioner and was assigned to family court. I found it a daunting task to make decisions that affected the very core of people's lives, particularly since the lifestyles and problems presented were often so far removed from my own experiences.

Every time I thought I'd heard it all before, litigants would appear, with such a tangled web of emotional ties and quirky circumstances, that I didn't know whether to laugh or cry, let alone how to determine their destiny.

Come with me to a chambers conference and a hearing on a motion for modification of child support:

"He only father of Charlie, Judge. Angie ain't even his. The D.A. can tell you. He's got two other cases goin' with two other chicks. He only decide to see the kids when the D.A. gone after him for support. He just harrassin' me." The tiny firebrand of a woman stops to take a breath.

"Mr. Taylor," I interject, "I understand you've shown up for supervised visits several times, but Mrs. Taylor didn't bring the children."

"Judge," he interrupts me, "Lashonda here, she on crack. She say she can't bring the kids for no supervised visits. Saturday's her day to have sex wit' her girlfriend. She want me to get 'em from her house. I'd pick 'em up from her but her ma's a bitch," he sighs.

"She done wave a semi-automatic in ma' face last time I seen her." Mr. Taylor stretches his 6-foot-3-inch frame in the chair, looking helpless, as the chambers conference continues.

"He can't come to ma' house, 'cause he peer in the windows," Lashonda Taylor throws in for good measure. "He stalk me all time. Anyhow, as I told ya last time, Judge, he can't take the kids to his house, 'cause he's got a boa constrictor he let run loose."

My job seems to be to figure out whether two children — a boy of four and a girl of three — should spend their Saturdays exposed to a boa constrictor or witness a crackhead having sex.

"Lashonda, the boa," Mr. Taylor says, his intense black eyes riveted on his ex. "Lashonda, the boa," he repeats to make sure I didn't miss the name, "lives in a tank."

"You bastard!" Mrs. Taylor spits out with venom worthy of her namesake.

I glance at the file from the Department of Social Services. Both parents have been investigated in connection with a child neglect case, but the court has not received the report because Mrs. Taylor refuses to sign a release.

"If you're worried about the snake, Mrs. Taylor, please release the DSS report so I can see it." I pass the release to her, and she signs without saying a word.

Does he really let the boa run loose? Is she on crack? Is Angie his child? I need that investigative report before making any changes in the visitation arrangements.

"I ain't comin' on Friday nights no more," Lashonda says, giving her ex a look that could shrivel a grape into a raisin. "We been havin' a bit a hanky-panky," she gives me a meaningful wink. "Damn you, sexy bastard. Excuse me, Judge. No more!" She spits at her former spouse. Divorced or not, it turns out the two have had a standing date for weekly sex.

"Enough," I say, raising my hand to stop her from continuing. "I'm leaving the order in place for supervised visits until I see the report from DSS." I stand to indicate that the conference is over.

"I ain't gonna father no more children, if I gotta support 'em but don't get to see 'em!" Mr. Taylor says in an intimidating tone.

If only he'd carry through with that threat.

He stomps out of my chambers.

As Mrs. Taylor heads for the door, she stops, turns and in a conspiratorial tone with unmistakable affection in her voice, says to me, "Ain't he cute, Judge?"

The next case on calendar is a motion to modify child support, brought by Antonio Morales. Antonio is representing himself. From his previous appearances I learned that his noble bearing reflects the fact that he is a descendent of a Spanish land grant family. He says his fortunes are dwindling. He claims that his reduced assets constitute the necessary change in circumstances, on which his request to lower the amount of support is based.

Antonio exudes sex appeal. His dark, intelligent eyes are sunk beneath bushy eyebrows, a high forehead and a head of curly black hair. His complexion is flawless. His lips are worthy of Clark Gable. He stands at the defendant's table with impeccable posture — square shoulders, flat stomach — and surveys the lineup of women to his left. His current wife is seated on his right. Two prior wives sit at the plaintiffs' table with the D.A., and an unidentified woman sits in no-man's-land, in the center of the courtroom between the two tables. All the women are good-looking Latinas, tall, slender and well dressed. Antonio looks them over with obvious satisfaction, like a couturier regarding his models at a fashion show.

The district attorney informs me that among the four women, Antonio has fathered eight female children, whom he is obligated to support.

"As you know, Judge, I was the Central American manager for a shipping company," Antonio reminds me.

"You will recall that the job ended when war broke out in El Salvador. I had been making $40,000 a year, a well-paid job at that time. There were lots of perks — housing, a cook, a maid and a chauffeur, hardship pay and so forth. Such hardship!" Antonio gives me a knowing smile. "Anyway, I digress," and he continues. "When I came back to San Francisco, I tried my hand at real estate for a year, without success." Antonio pauses and sighs.

"You see how beautiful they all are," Antonio says, making a gesture with his hands in the direction of the women, as though their beauty explained everything. "I married them, one at a time, when they got pregnant. All except Maria Alvarez," and he nods toward the woman in the middle. "They all begged me to bring them to America."

I see that Mr. Morales' financial declaration shows he owns a home in Menlo Park, which — based on a 1995 assessed valuation — he claims is worth $860,000. He has a one-quarter interest in his mother's home, located in Atherton, valued at $4 million. He owns a half interest in a vacant lot on a steep hillside in Atherton, value unknown. His financial declaration indicates that the site has building restrictions and there is neighborhood opposition to development.

I note the D.A. has not done his homework regarding the value of that lot, nor has he given me any information regarding Mr. Morales' past earnings or present earning potential.

"I inherited $2 million in 1981, when my father died, and haven't worked since. When we were last in court, you set support based on the income I then had from the two million. I'm paying $900 a month for each of the three children not living with me. During the recession, Judge, I burned up half the capital, trying to support four households. There's only a million left now."

"It takes $11,000 a month just to keep the seven of us going," the current wife interjects.

I think Mr. Morales has been busy fathering more daughters. There are five girls in his household.

"Judge," the D.A. chimes in, "Mr. Morales could consider going back to work. These women aren't asking for an increase, but they live on a couple of thousand a month with their daughters, while the five children living with Mr. Morales and his wife live in Menlo Park and share $11,000 a month.

"Let me point out, Judge, that each household has a 12-year-old daughter," the D.A. continues, with a hint of amusement. "The expenses for those children must be very similar."

"Is there some reason that you are not working, Mr. Morales?" I inquire.

"I manage the investments, Your Honor," he replies. "I lost money doing real estate and have no marketable skills. I'm almost 50 years old. What can I do?"

For a fleeting moment I consider recommending a move to Utah, where he could gather his harem under one roof, thus reducing his expenses.

Alas, reality intervenes so I continue the hearing for three months and tell Mr. Morales to go to the Employment Development Department for evaluation and job search. I tell him I may consider attributing income to him if he makes no real efforts to find a job. I tell him he may want to consider turning his assets over to a professional financial manager.

The women all beam at Mr. Morales as the hearing ends. It must be nice to have his kind of charm.

*One day, I received the ultimate accolade
from a young couple who had appeared
before me the week before:*

"I want you to know that me
and my friend named our
dog after you."

CHRISTMAS VISITATION

"Mr. Frazier," I said, glaring over my glasses at Mrs. Trafalgar's attorney, "please tell me we are not here to talk about the custody of a pig?"

"I'm afraid so, Your Honor," Mr. Frazier replied. "You see …"

My mind wandered. Having presided in family court for a couple of years, I had come to dread the holiday season, when decibel levels rise in parents' voices and general hysteria prevails over the subject of children's upcoming vacations.

The case preceding the Trafalgars' had involved a child named Jason. Was he to be with Dad on Christmas Eve this year or on Christmas morning? If it was Christmas Eve, Mom wanted to pick up the four-year-old from Dad's house a minute past midnight. That's Christmas Day, isn't it? she had contended.

I spent many a December day trying but failing to sort through similarly earthshaking problems. I thought I'd seen it all, but I must admit the Trafalgars' case had a unique flavor.

"You see," Frazier was saying as my mind returned to the subject at hand, "during a period of reconciliation, my client and Mr. Trafalgar acquired a Spanish pig, which they treat as though he were a dog."

This appeared to be the type of divorce in which only the very wealthy can indulge, a bitter five-year battle to divide their community property. After they separated for the second time, Henry and Veronica had an Order to Show Cause hearing. The judge to whom the case was assigned lost patience with the vitriolic interruptions of the proceedings by the couple. The judge refused to take testimony on the subject of the family pet and ordered the attorneys to earn their keep and work out the problem without court intervention.

After some 16 hours of billable time for each cream-of-the-crop family law specialist, a temporary arrangement was worked out. They agreed that El Mundo, the porker/dog, was to travel back and forth between the parents' vacation residences. El Mundo would spend a week with Veronica in her splendid home at Silverado Country Club, in Napa Valley, reveling in his walks along the golf course. He would stay alternate weeks with Henry at a West Marin County estate. The temporary arrangement provided that the pig/dog would be driven between his two homes by a liveried chauffeur in the back of a Mercedes station wagon.

The decision as to which of the Trafalgars would occupy which summer home had been a piece of cake, compared to the problem of who would have temporary custody of El Mundo. Months later, to what must have been the great joy of the judge who presided over the dissolution case, El Mundo's permanent custody was determined by a settlement agreement. His "dad" gave up custody, retaining visitation rights, in exchange for an antique Jaguar sedan he coveted.

Veronica's elation at having won the custody battle became somewhat diminished when the reality of sole custody set in. She continued El Mundo's routine as best she could, feeding the pig milk and biscuits, washing him with shampoo, and teaching him to sit on his haunches. However, due to his enormous size, El Mundo became a bit of a problem underfoot. His habit of climbing up on Veronica's bed didn't seem quite as cute now that the teensy-weensy bundle had grown to 200 pounds. After consulting with an architect in Sonoma, Veronica had a palatial pigsty constructed and moved El Mundo out of the house.

Henry never came to visit. As the weeks passed, it became clear that El Mundo missed his dad. The pig's appetite diminished and he developed a nervous rash. He fell into a monthlong depression. Visits to the veterinary psychiatrist in Santa Rosa yielded no progress.

In late November, when Veronica appeared in my court again, I was a bit nonplussed when I heard her request that Henry be ordered to visit El Mundo for Christmas and that he pick up the cost of the porker-shrink, the architect and the construction. Henry, though not present at the hearing, through his lawyer, Thomas Pickering, assured me that his client would remedy El Mundo's depression by Christmas. With a well-timed glance toward heaven, as if seeking divine assistance, Pickering pledged that he would work something out regarding the bills. I was happy to abdicate having to make a decision.

I must admit, I thought of El Mundo that Christmas, visualizing him among the animals when I took my grandchildren to view the manger scene at Grace Cathedral, but otherwise put the matter out of my mind.

The following January, I ran into Henry Trafalgar's attorney at a Bar Association function. He related that his client had delivered a female pig to his ex-wife's house on Christmas morning and last he heard, El Mundo had assumed the proper role of mate, cavorting around in the dirt with his sweetheart, refusing to stand on his hind legs and generally acting like a happy pig. He retains only one vestige of his former life as a dog and still refuses to settle down at bedtime until Veronica kisses him goodnight. I uttered a non-judicious "yuck" when I heard that.

❋   ❋   ❋

May all your Christmas visitation problems be light.

Many people call me "Aggie." I like to think it was just a typo and not a comment on my eating habits when a litigant sent me a note, which had me laughing so hard, it sent tears streaming down my face:

"Hy, Assie Hogg,

I was at San Francisco and my car went out of gas and then I puch it to the grong parking play, becouse I don't find the right street. And my car is havy also and I was alone. I no! Ther is no problem for you, but I saw the officer puting the tiket at my car and I tell him, please let me put my gallon of gas first and let me go, and he don't answerd me, then he toll me is not my problem, OK?"

DISASTER PREPAREDNESS 101

When I learned that an issue of San Francisco Attorney Magazine would be devoted to the topic of disaster preparedness, I thought about how differently people react to disasters.

In World War II, during the Siege of Budapest in the winter of 1944-1945, the apartment house where my family lived was hit by an incendiary bomb, trapping the building's residents in the basement shelter. The ensuing fire made it impossible to reach the street, but some of the residents could still run upstairs to attempt to rescue some items from their apartments. A rather corpulent lady from apartment 3-D came staggering back down the stairs to the shelter, burdened by the weight of a hideous lamp with a garish red shade. She was pursued down the stairs by billowing smoke. Lesson 101: What not to do in a fire.

Meg, the 23-year-old granddaughter of a friend of mine, was traveling in China for three months, studying Mandarin. One day, she called home, sobbing on the phone. She had traveled on an overnight train, jammed on the third bunk of a three-bunk compartment and arrived, after a miserable night, in Shanghai in pouring rain. She had called on her cell phone, standing outside the station, soaked to the skin, lugging her suitcase, unable to make herself understood by a taxi driver so she could get a ride to her cousin's home. Meg's dad, Rob, who is Chinese-American, told her to stay on the line. He got on his cell phone and called his mother. Meg's grandmother is a San Francisco resident who speaks

Cantonese, the dialect spoken in Shanghai. He patched Grandma through to Meg's cell phone. Grandma told Meg to put the reluctant cab driver on the phone. Grandma, from San Francisco, then read the riot act in Cantonese to the cabbie in Shanghai, instructing him in no uncertain terms to deliver Meg to her cousin's home. Lesson 102: When all else fails, call home.

Which reminds me that we once had a call from one of our offspring. He had just moved to Los Angeles and was calling from the side of a freeway, wanting to know what to do with a flat tire. Lesson 103: Do not fix flats on the freeway — call AAA.

Returning to my wartime experiences, during the siege of Budapest, Hungary, my sister and I, who were 10 and eight respectively, can report that if your flashlight battery gives out in an emergency, you can supply a bit of uric acid to extend its life for a few minutes. When we were hungry and wanted to con the occupying German troops out of a chocolate bar or some other treat, we would offer to extend the life of their burned out flashlights. We'd squat behind their jeeps, pee on the batteries and voilà, life returned. We'd grab our reward and then run like mad, before the light fizzled out again. Lesson 104?

NOT EXACTLY SUGARPLUMS

If the visions of Christmas in your head are of little lambs, a cow and an ass nestled near the Baby Jesus, count your blessings.

My head is filled with bizarre memories. There was a time when our home was inhabited by four children under seven, all of whom — were they young today in the 21st century — would no doubt be called hyperactive and put on Ritalin. "All is calm" was not a lyric I sang with conviction.

During the month between Thanksgiving and Christmas, the children's anticipation of Santa's coming reached a fever pitch. Pointing at items in the Sears Toy Catalog — which in those days constituted Santa's bible — various children's voices would demand, as they grabbed the book back and forth: "Give me it." "I gotta have it." "No you don't." "I'm gonna tell Santa you hit me."

I must say that in Hungary, where I was raised, parents were smarter than my husband and I. There, we children hung our stockings the night before St. Nicholas' Feast Day, December 7. The stockings were either filled with candy or, if the children's past behavior had been less than perfect, a switch would be sticking out of the sock in the morning, courtesy of St. Nick. The appearance of this instrument of torture gave fair warning that a child's conduct had to improve, or the Christ Child would leave nothing under the tree on Christmas Eve. This tradition, of course, had been invented to control the behavior of kids between December 7 and Christmas.

But I digress. No switches would have controlled the chaos at our San Francisco home when my husband and I were raising our little angels in the 1960s. A Siamese cat — Aristotle — and a Cockapoo — Snuffy — increased the turmoil.

Aristotle loved Christmas as much as the children did. The brighter the ornament, the better he liked it. One year, much to our darlings' delight and his own, Aristotle batted low-hanging ornaments on our tree until they crashed to the floor. The next year, we moved the shining balls up where he couldn't reach the fragile ones, or so we thought. The darn cat took up ballet. We watched him leap three feet into the air, pirouette, pause in mid-air, twist his entire body, and bat down the object of his affections.

My husband and I thought we'd outsmarted Aristotle the following year when we decorated with Styrofoam, papier-maché and other indestructible ornaments. However, Aristotle took a running start across the living room, ran up the bark of the 8-foot tree and perched himself delicately on top of the star at the pinnacle. The tree swayed back and forth. I swear Aristotle smiled as the tree rocked, enjoying the ride, before the whole thing came crashing down, much to the delight of the assembled children.

One year, I thought Aristotle finally got what was coming to him. He had a habit of flopping on his back on top of a basket full of laundry in the kitchen, pretending to be asleep. If Snuffy, our dog, made the mistake of sauntering past, Aristotle would reach out and scratch him, sending the poor dog yelping and whimpering through the apartment. On this particular December day though, the cat miscalculated, and his claws became caught in the dog's curly black fur. Snuffy took off, hoping to shake Aristotle loose, dragging the cat along, the remaining three cat legs flying, as he splayed on Snuffy's back.

A cheering section of kids made way for the racing pair as they approached the living room. It was at this point that the long-suffering Snuffy stopped dead in his tracks and shook himself as though he'd just come in from the rain. This maneuver had the desired result, sending the cat flying. Aristotle, as was his wont, landed on all fours and, for a second or two, actually looked a bit dazed. Then he executed a classic cat maneuver. He sat very erect and still for a moment, then slowly lifted his right paw to his mouth, licked it and began grooming himself behind his right ear. He gave us all a very dismissive stare, as if to say, "Nothing happened, you stupid people — nothing at all."

May your cat lounge in front of the fire this Christmas!

"Dear, dear, I got ticket parking, but I can't pay because I didn't get nothing right now. I know I had mistake. I want to pay but I don't have work. I don't have money.

Last month I'm borrowed my friends car, came to do green card at San Francisco. I think dear, dear, you will understand me. I'm sorry about that. You are consider about me please, dear."

(Dear, oh dear. I'm an immigrant, too. I do understand!)

THE ARMPIT OF THE LAW

Career paths are chosen for many reasons. In the 1950s, a friend of mine became a dentist because the line to register for medical school was longer and he didn't feel like waiting. Some become lawyers because of early exposure to stories about Clarence Darrow or because they watched Perry Mason in their youth. Others go to law school because their mothers or fathers are lawyers; some study law because they are Jewish and don't want to become a doctor. Some people go to law school because they want to save the world. I wish I could say I had been driven by noble motives.

Had I listened to wiser heads, I could have saved myself from a convoluted path. But in that case, I could just as well have ended up as a mortician: In 1954, as a high school senior, I took extensive tests at Stanford, the results of which showed that I had a high aptitude for law, with a potential career as an undertaker a close second.

Those who labor in family law will see that I ultimately found my true calling. Whenever a client recited the woes of his or her marriage, I could adapt a funereal look of sympathy worthy of an undertaker, while at the same time, offer sage legal advice.

I often felt genuine empathy for a new client, who related the cruelties he or she had experienced at the hands of a mate. After offering proper condolences and suggesting legal approaches, all of which were met by answers from the client amounting to "Yes, but …," the client would reveal that he or she had, in fact, been chewing over events that had happened many years prior to our meeting.

One divorcée handed me her ex-husband's death certificate tucked into a pile of pleadings, indicating that he died 15 years prior to our conversation. She had wanted me to conjure up child support from beyond the grave. Such situations sometimes made me envy undertakers, who have the corpse for a client.

However, at the time of the vocational aptitude test, I didn't give either law or undertaking a second's thought. In those days, both were considered male occupations. Home and school had programmed me to understand that if I had the misfortune to be unwed when I finished college, I was to kill time until Prince Charming came along by being a secretary, nurse or a teacher.

While in college, a part-time job led me to become a legal secretary. After working for an attorney who represented wayward clerics and illegal Hungarian border-crossers, I moved on to my hot-air phase, taking dictation about natural gas contracts.

I plowed my way through various law offices. In one office, I typed patent descriptions of machines that the inventor intended to enhance the process of the artificial insemination of cows. Not long afterward, when the invention failed, I drew up pleadings, putting the inventor through bankruptcy.

It took a number of years and then, a tape I had been transcribing motivated me to head for law school. When I heard one of my bosses' dictation over the sound of his urinating, it occurred to me that if I waited for that knight in shining armor, I might well end up spending my life cleaning up after the horse.

I wish I could claim I went to law school because I was struck by a burning desire to do justice. Instead, it was a personal injury law firm in Seattle that finally pushed me over the edge. This firm was the last straw.

Working in the armpit of the law had its memorable moments. When I arrived at work in the mornings, the firm's waiting room would usually be filled with faces peering out of cervical collars. These devices were standard equipment, handed out by emergency crews at accident scenes. The clients arrived at the office by the station wagonload, delivered by an ambulance chaser who had recruited them in emergency rooms. She received a kickback when each case she referred, settled.

Some days, uniform-clad bus drivers lined the walls in the lobby, waiting their turn to see a lawyer and relate their workers compensation claims. The firm had a legendary reputation for being able to make a silk purse out of a sow's ear, as far as the facts of an accident were concerned. Never mind that the driver had run over a pedestrian's foot while the victim was standing on the curb, or that a driver had used his bus as a battering ram against a VW. My employers could have him come out smelling like a rose.

The firm's receptionist, Dana Sanctus, carried plastic-wrapped flies in her purse. When she ran short of cash, she would surreptitiously deposit one in an unsuspecting restaurant's luncheon salad. She then would raise a ruckus, demanding to see the manager. Lunch, of course, would be on the house. Afterward, Ms. Sanctus would return to the office, where she wrote her own demand letter on office letterhead, claiming ptomaine poisoning from having eaten the tainted food. She'd present her letter to one of the partners for signature and mail it a few days later, with medical bills and a wage loss statement, to the restaurant's insurance carrier.

Insurance adjusters were wined and dined on a routine basis under the guise of settlement discussions, which helped to oil the negotiations. When funds in the firm's coffers ran low, a telephone call to the most recently greased adjuster netted the desired result.

The firm had shystering down to such a science that in my years in their employ, I do not recall more than two cases going to trial. Nor was there ever a way to prove that anything untoward was going on.

I'm not sure if it was the fly in the salad or the day when one of the attorneys announced that he had founded a church, but one of those events was the straw that broke this camel's back and sent me scurrying to law school.

He had received a mail order diploma from Arizona with a guarantee of legal representation, should the IRS question the legitimacy of his ministry. He made himself pastor, his wife his assistant and his infant son the secretary. Henceforth, he planned to funnel his income through the church.

The senior partner, sorry he hadn't thought of that particular ploy first, could hardly wait to follow his partner into holy mail-order religion. Alas, fate intervened, and he died before he had set up his congregation.

Though tempted by the thought of a career in undertaking, I signed up for night law school.

FOR WHOM PRO BONO TOLLS

I once had a case that followed the usual pattern where, because the clients were receiving legal services for free, they used inordinate hours of attorney time. There were no children involved in the divorce and the parties had divided their meager community property when they separated. However, correspondence with opposing counsel deteriorated to exchanges regarding the fate of the one red lamp still jointly owned and coveted by both parties.

The opposing counsel sent me a poetic letter urging my client, the wife, to relinquish her claim to the bordello-style illumination. Counsel managed to draw the subject out to fourteen paragraphs, describing the lamp, its value — sentimental and monetary — and including a demand to settle the case or proceed to trial by a date two weeks from the date of his letter.

Neatly placed within the folds of his letter, I found a lavender index card on which a single immortal word appeared, emblazoned in block letters stamped by the husband's attorney: BULLSHIT!

During my legal career — aside from handling pro bono cases — I participated in innumerable pro bono community activities. I spoke at Law Day at a Festival for Justice held at Hunters Point and trained paralegals in a program at San Francisco State University. I also taught street law at Downtown High School, addressed the Filipino American Socialization Association on legal rights, and supervised attorneys at numerous restraining order clinics offered by the Bar Association. I served on the advisory board of Elizabeth Fry Center, worked with prisoner mothers, and also served on the advisory board of Richmond Hills Center for the homeless. I arbitrated fee disputes between attorneys and their clients, and volunteered on community board panels. However, these pro bono activities were all overshadowed by that one red lamp and that lavender index card!

The originator of that succinct piece of humor eventually went on to prosecute for the State Bar in discipline cases. At one point, he represented the State Bar against former San Francisco Mayor Joe Alioto. Joe had an uncanny way of facing the press at the end of a day's hearing and uttering a headline-grabbing phrase, slanting the day's news coverage his way, to the frustration of the prosecutor.

On the fifth day of the hearings, after giving the matter a good deal of thought, the State Bar's lawyer finally managed to snag a headline and be quoted favorably in the next day's *Chronicle*. When I saw his name in the paper, I delighted in recalling his red lamp settlement letter. I clipped the article from the *Chron*, folded the BULLSHIT card in it and mailed it back to its author.

For 10 years, I spent four hours a week, plus one overnight a month, answering the hotline at Suicide Prevention. A great majority of the calls involved chatting with people whom the volunteers called "the regulars," lonesome folks who whiled away the night hours by calling us. Suicide Prevention even kept index cards on some of these people, naming them and identifying their stories, and advising the volunteers how to handle their calls expeditiously.

Most shifts were akin to military service — hours of boredom, punctuated by moments of terror when someone's life might hang in the balance if I, as a volunteer, couldn't come up with the proper words to deter a would-be suicide. Pro bono publico can come in varied guises. I wonder if among the publico anyone would consider saving a lawyer's life a pro bono activity?

On one of my overnight stints, a man who identified himself as Henry, an alcoholic lawyer, phoned from the Suicide Prevention call box on the Golden Gate Bridge. Our Suicide Prevention directive was to page a staff member whenever we heard from a genuinely suicidal caller. Henry whispered that he was leaning over the railing as we talked.

I immediately paged Shirley, the staff person on call that night. In a few minutes, one of the other volunteers alerted me that Shirley was waiting for me on another line. After receiving Henry's promise to keep talking, I handed off the suicidal lawyer to the volunteer, while I conferred with Shirley. I discussed the particulars of Henry's problems with her and received some sound advice on how to proceed with his call.

I alerted the Golden Gate Bridge authorities about the would-be jumper before getting back on the line with Henry. I applied Shirley's advice to our continued conversation and managed to calm the caller and have him back away from the bridge railing. Henry surrendered quietly and walked off the bridge with a highway patrol officer, who came on the line briefly to tell me that everything was OK.

The hotline rang again, immediately after I had hung up. This Shirley — sounding quite different from the way she had a few minutes earlier — was on the line, wanting to know why I had paged her. It took a few minutes of earnest conversation for the two of us to untangle what had just taken place. It seemed that the Shirley who had given me the sage advice — in proper social worker jargon — on how to handle Henry's suicidal urge, turned out to be one of our "regulars," a client who had spent many hours in the past talking to numerous volunteers. She had learned to speak suicide preventionese fluently.

Lawyer Henry will never know who saved his life that night!

Ever since that incident, I've wondered whether we couldn't just devise a system where the hotline callers could be patched to the "regulars" by their profiles, thus creating a whole army of pro bono volunteers.

"I am paying this fine since it seems to be the easy way out. But I strongly suggest that the meter, which I parked in front of, should be properly labeled. Please send a meter maid by to check it out. On the front it only says 4:00 p.m. to 6:00 p.m. Well, I am stupid and from Stockton, so that's two strikes against me, but I really thought it meant you could park there between 4:00 p.m. and 6:00 p.m. It was 4:15 when we parked. Now, I thought it was strange, but we were in San Francisco. It's a strange place to me." (Nancy Dean)

Ms. Dean's letter reminded me of one I received from Aberdeen, South Dakota, some time ago, enclosing a photograph of a pole festooned with five different instructions regulating parking: No parking 1:00 a.m. to 6:00 a.m. Tuesday Street Cleaning; No Double Parking; Emergency Snow Route; 2 Hour Limit 8:00 a.m. to 6:00 p.m. And, lastly, the one that summed it all up: No Parking This Side.

And Ms. Dean thinks San Francisco is strange!

A CHILD IS BORN

Photos of two strikingly beautiful women stood in identical frames on Judge Abrams' desk. Neither resembled anyone in the family photo, which had a prominent place on the bookcase. Who were these women? During all the years I practiced in the judge's court, I never did find out.

Some judges' chambers give clues to a life outside the courthouse. Most often, for the men, the objects are sports-related and, for the women, child-centered. At times though, they give hints to passions I would never have guessed.

I remember meeting a big bear of a man, Judge Diamond, years ago, in a one-room courthouse in rural Lake County. In a corner of his chambers, he had a shelf where a menagerie of the most delicate glass animals imaginable was on display.

No one ever asked me about the picture of the wrinkled, scrawny baby tucked into a corner of the blotter on my desk. I'd catch attorneys glancing at it and averting their eyes, perhaps afraid that the baby depicted a menopausal folly. Many years later, my memory of her still casts a shadow on my holidays.

A 2-pound, 5-ounce toothpick of a baby had been born at San Francisco General Hospital the previous night. In the predawn darkness, the muted lights of the nursery camouflaged the bustling activity.

For three years, I'd been going there as a volunteer every Tuesday morning, from 5 a.m. until it was time to go to my real job at 9. The nurses trained me and kept an eye on my handling of their diminutive charges. For the past year or so, I'd been allowed to help in the Critical Care Unit, which housed the sickest and most fragile newborns.

Baby Bailey, just five hours old, had taken up residence under a heating lamp, on a high-tech table. She was trussed like a turkey, with dripping IV, a tube, which seemed wider than her leg, down her throat, oxygen hissing into her body. Her translucent skin appeared stretched over her limbs. Her tiny hands on her skeletal arms were as small as my thumbnail. She gave new meaning to the term "bag of bones," and yet, Baby Bailey was a perfect human being.

Though the child's a girl, Ann, the nurse in charge, dubbed her Billie, from that old song, "Bill Bailey, Won't You Please Come Home."

Not so simple, little Bailey. If all the nurturing care pulls you through, where and what will home be? Your mama, age 16, dropped you into our fine world at midnight, almost four months too soon. Your home will not likely be with her. If the fates have been good to you, maybe you have a good grandma. One, who anguished over the loss of her daughter to the drug culture, will want to take you in and love you. If you're not so lucky, you may end up in a foster home, where someone may or may not love you.

For now you look crucified on the table, but I see that you are a survivor and active. Your cries are pitiful, because they are muffled by the tube down your throat. Who knows what all is dripping into you, to make you believe you are still nourished by your mama. When I stroke your arm, your skin feels like the finest silk, your bones beneath like the most fragile china.

A week has gone by, and your mama has not named you. She is still in the ward adjoining the nursery. The doctors are trying to ease her withdrawal from drugs. She never comes to see you. They say she cursed her way through your delivery. She throws things at the nurses, because her young body constantly craves more drugs.

No, little Bailey, you will not be going home with her. You have been moved to an incubator, still trussed but breathing on your own, unaware of your uncertain future. Each day, the finest that medicine can do is being done for you, and you are gaining weight. Suffering from withdrawal, you still shudder and sneeze from time to time. The doctors try to decrease the opium that helps you through your spasms. Withdraw from your mama, too, while you are at it, little Bailey.

The next day, at my real job, I preside in family court over a monumental custody battle. The mother of the child involved, when she testifies, insists on showing me a picture of the baby who is the center of the controversy. She is a poppy-cheeked little girl. Her antique crib and elegant bedding reflect the trappings of a child of privilege. I can't help but think of Billie, fragile and vulnerable at the hospital, who doesn't even have a name.

At home on Thursday evening, I run across a picture of my youngest son, taken at St. Mary's Hospital the day he was born. He looks three times the size of Baby Bailey. I'm anxious to see the tiny girl.

I return to the hospital after another week has passed and head straight for Billie's section of the nursery. Where is Baby Bailey? She's not in her incubator. For a moment my heart stops. Did she die while I was gone?

"She graduated," Nurse Ann tells me, pointing to one of the open simulator beds. Ann, wearing a ceramic stork pinned to her uniform, lights up the room with her smile.

Bailey is sleeping on her side, between two sausage-shaped pillows and is swaddled like a third little sausage. The bed is undulating to give her the feel of being inside the womb. It makes a thumping sound like her mama's heart and is supposed to calm and soothe and help with withdrawal. Sleep, little Bailey, sleep. A cruel world awaits you.

The phone is ringing. Nurse Jeanette, who holds and rocks Billie every chance she gets, answers, then holds the phone away from her ear. Those of us near her can hear a string of profanities coming over the line.

It's Bailey's mom. She was discharged a week ago and wants to know when she can take her baby home. In between curses, she giggles, obviously high. She wants her baby.

Jeanette, her voice strained, tries to explain that the baby is still very sick, still withdrawing. She hangs up the phone, goes over and pats Baby Bailey gently on the head. I note that the pink card displayed on little Bailey's simulator still shows no first name.

Another week and it is Christmas. Little Bailey is much on my mind. When I walk into the nursery, Millie, a diminutive nurse, fussing over her charges, says, "Bailey's got a name. Go and see."

I wonder why she doesn't just tell me what it is. Baby Bailey is whimpering in her undulating cocoon. I gently pick her up, to quiet her, and say good morning. She's still connected to monitors and has one IV, but if I am careful not to disconnect anything, I can hold her. She feels and looks more and more like my own babies did when they were newly born. Her bones are no longer visible through her skin. I've fallen in love with Baby Bailey and wish I could take her home and raise her.

She wears a jaunty, yellow knit cap to keep her head warm. Around the edges she's beginning to sprout tiny black corkscrew curls. What's to become of you, Baby?

"Merry Christmas, little Bailey," I whisper.

Doctors, in their infinite wisdom, tell me that newborns don't smile. Perhaps it is a grimace caused by gas or just a nervous twitch, but I prefer to believe that she is responding to my greeting: she smiles.

I glance at the name card on her crib and summing up Baby Bailey's present, past and more than likely future, I see that her mama has named her "Irish Cream Bailey."

I wonder how she's doing this Christmas.

THROUGH THE LOOKING GLASS

Theresa peered at her image in a hand-held mirror she had drawn out of the over-sized bag at her feet. She sat on the beat-up couch in the dilapidated anteroom to the women's restroom. The ladies' room on the second floor of the Hall of Justice was a few doors down the corridor from my courtroom, so my staff and I shared it with the public.

Theresa had introduced herself to me on a prior occasion when we had stood in front of the paper towel dispenser. Many of the prostitutes who frequented that bathroom were on a first-name basis with the clerks from my court and me. They regarded us as the benign residents of traffic court, as compared to the judges who wielded justice in the criminal courts, around which the women's daily fortunes revolved.

Theresa was a not-infrequent overnight guest of the sheriff. I assumed that, along with other ladies of the night, she had just been OR'd (released on her own recognizance) from an arraignment court.

"Whoever invented stretch cloth, must've had us hookers in mind, honey," she said to me as she moved her mirror so it reflected her voluptuous shape. "Not only can I wiggle into this get-up in five minutes, but even better, pull it off in 30 seconds flat. If you'll pardon the expression — flat I ain't." She glanced down at her ample cleavage as she said this. Theresa wore one of those short, purple numbers with shoestring straps; most of her behind hung out.

"Mmm," I mumbled, heading for one of the cubicles. A few minutes later, when I emerged, Theresa was still sitting on the couch, straightening her fishnet stockings. She stood up, pulled in her stomach, threw her shoulders back and sashayed over to stand next to me at an adjacent sink, to get a better look at herself in a bigger mirror.

"I got this at St. Anthony's Thrift Store." She smoothed her skintight dress over her stomach and paused, before adding a critical appraisal. "Don't think St. Anthony would like it."

"I like purple," I told her, trying to be diplomatic.

"This stretchy stuff's even comfortable to sleep in, which is what I was tryin' to do last night," she informed me. "Geez, I wish they'd pipe down in those cells. I told 'em to cut the racket. I asked 'em nicely. I was tryin' to sleep! 'Say please!' they yelled back at me.

"You know, Louise, the redhead?"

"Yes, I know who you mean." Louise was also a regular morning apparition in the bathroom.

"She eggs 'em on. No use arguin' with that bitch — she's nothin' but trouble. I had to stick my head under the pillow to block the noise. You'd think I'd be used to it by now. I'm in there couple nights a week.

"Last night, they stuck me in the holding pen with four other girls, for hours. They picked me up in a sweep in front of that 24-hour strip joint on Eddy Street. Just my luck. Damn cruiser came by right when I was giving this John a blow job, leaning into his car on the driver's side. Bastard cop, he come up behind me and rub his dick on my ass, before he grab my arms and cuff me. He piss me off, so I kick him but good in the shin with my spiked heels." She glanced down and swiveled her ankle, so I could see her shoes.

"'Damn you, bitch!' that cop hollered at me, and twists the cuffs too tight, on purpose. The John took off down Eddy Street, and the cop didn't even bother to get the car license." Theresa shook her head, while applying blue shadow around her eyes as she spoke. Her eyes reminded me of those of a newborn — deep, dark, ocean blue.

I edged my way toward the exit, since it was almost time for the morning session in my courtroom to resume. I loved these encounters with a world so different from my own, so I uttered another non-committal "hmm," to keep her talking and leaned against the wall by the door.

"Geez, you wouldn't believe how the pillows stink in that place. Not enough the whole place smell like pee and Clorox, but they can't even give us clean pillows. Shit, those bitches sure can act up. They were just harassin' me 'cause I'm purtier than they are." Theresa continued to regard her image in the glass, adjusting a strand of her matted, reddish-gold hair. "They kept clangin' the bars and pullin' their spoons across 'em," she continued. "I couldn't sleep a wink, even with the pillow over my head.

"I kept thinking all night, hoping in the morning I'd get that runt of a P.D., you know, that little Mexican dude with the mustache."

"Yeh," I said and smiled inwardly at her description of Public Defender Ramirez. I made a mental note to tell him about my bathroom encounter, next time I saw him.

"He's great at sweet-talking the judge and tellin' him what a tough life I've had. I was hoping to be outta here, before you know it, having my Egg McMuffin next door. And that's just what happened."

Theresa smacked her lips, to distribute the purple lipstick she'd just applied to match her dress. She winked at me in the mirror with a self-satisfied expression on her face. She was trying hard to make herself look young, though she was 40, if she's a day.

"And them three shitheads in the cell last night will be guests of the sheriff for a while longer in this place, 'cause they drew that know-nothing, silver-spoon P.D.

from Harvard, and the judge gave 'em 30 days. Who says there ain't no justice in this world?

"Thanks for listening to me, honey," she said, taking one last appreciative look at herself in the mirror. "See ya."

She swung the door wide open and strutted down the corridor toward the elevators. As she walked, she looked back over her shoulder, gave me a big smile and said, "What a funny world."

On the back page of the next day's *Chronicle*, a headline over a single paragraph caught my eye:

Prostitute's Death in the Tenderloin Probed.

I continued to read:

San Francisco police were investigating the death of a known prostitute whose nude body was found early yesterday morning on a Tenderloin sidewalk. Several of the responding officers said they recognized the victim as Theresa Bryan.

SUNRISE IN SAN FRANCISCO

"A little sodomy, a bit of oral copulation, a suicide dive: It's sunrise in San Francisco." That's how my notes read one morning, after I'd spent the night issuing Emergency Protective Orders in domestic violence cases. I often wrote comments when half asleep and the next morning, would be surprised at what I had written. I thought the notation a bit bizarre when I read it, until I looked over what had gone on during my 16-hour shift, on duty answering the phone while the court was closed.

5:14 p.m. A non-student visiting his ex-girlfriend at San Francisco State attempted suicide by jumping out a fifth-floor dormitory window. He staggered to his feet, punched out a would-be rescuer and headed for the roof of the parking structure, where he was prevented from jumping again by a security guard.

Reporting officer stated the guy was 5150 (detained on a 72-hour psychiatric hold), but said he wanted his ex-girlfriend to die with him in his next attempt. He had tried pills and slit his wrists in the past.

I hope the threat against the girlfriend will keep him hospitalized past the three-day limit so he can get the help he needs.

10:46 p.m. Woman at shelter with three children reported that her husband performed oral copulation on her eight-year-old boy from a prior relationship. Physical exam of child revealed bloody penis.

Some calls made me wish for the existence of hell!

2:03 a.m. Sodomy accusation and arrest. Suspect, after being thrown out of apartment by relatives of the victim, came back and tried to kick his way through the kitchen door. His foot broke through and got stuck. Arresting officer cuffed him, then had fire department cut him out of door.

3:53 a.m. Aunt reported that her nephew was acting crazy and had thrown cold water on her while she slept. Arresting officer reported that when he arrived at the house the suspect was refusing to come out from under a desk, insisting that HE is the president of the United States.

"Someone should tell Bush and Gore," my notes said. This occurred during the time the Supreme Court was deciding who had been elected president.

* * *

I glanced over my notes from the previous couple of weeks, and it struck me that there is no limit to the weapons of choice used in domestic violence cases.

A husband and wife argued; she jabbed her finger up his nose.

A boyfriend threatened his girlfriend with his barbells.

Man whipped woman with a belt.

Woman hit man with her shoe.

Fiancé threw the remote at her.

Couple went at each other with machetes and knives.

Spouses spit on each other.

Wife hit husband with a stick.

Girlfriend threw 40-ounce bottle of beer at girlfriend.

Housemate threatened to drive car into house while roommate slept.

She threw anything not tied down: He got hit with salad bowl, meat cleaver. Officer said victim needs an Emergency Protective Order and a new girlfriend.

I like it when a cop retains his sense of humor.

●   ●   ●

Why do they do it?

She wouldn't sign the settlement agreement.

Someone parked in their driveway.

Argued over sex: He's lousy, she stinks.

He kicked the dog, she went to its defense.

She threatened to kill doctor, because he left her with a scar after successful cancer surgery.

He threw out her teeth. Neighbors said she routinely beat him up.

She brought home the 16th cat.

Soup was too hot.

Wife took care of husband who was unable to walk without help of a walker. He belittled her constantly, ordering her around. Threw walker at her. Tried to strangle her after getting out of wheelchair and walking on his own. He surprised himself so much, his heart started racing. He called paramedics. Taken to nursing home temporarily.

He loved the bird more than he loved his boyfriend.

●   ●   ●

Over time I've learned to keep the nightly mayhem at arm's length. However, the phone calls that still manage to truly upset me often involve violence against children, or people in authority or trust giving incredibly bad advice to the victims of domestic violence:

Call to police by friend of victim. Victim had been stalked everywhere she went by violent ex-husband. Victim told by spiritual adviser not to report ex to police because ex-husband had "evil powers" he might turn on her. Friend refused to testify about the stalking. She also feared evil powers.

Unreported prior rape came to the attention of the police after the husband beat the wife to a pulp. She claimed she kept it to herself because her pastor told her all marriages have problems; that she should work through those problems; that it is her Christian duty to have sex on demand.

❋   ❋   ❋

Once in a great while, someone gets what's coming to him, without any help from the system of justice:

Officer responding to 911 call from victim of severe beating heard male screaming in back yard; found suspect, who had been attempting to flee, skewered on barbed wire fence.

EUREKA

It seems I am forever on the wrong side of the law.

Recently I traveled from San Francisco to Osaka, Japan with a layover at Narita Airport in Tokyo. At the security check in San Francisco and Tokyo and at customs in Osaka, I was pulled out of line, told to take my shoes off, patted down and wanded. In Japan, the instructions included being told to put on some slippers while they searched me.

When packing for the return trip, I used *space bags*, which squeeze the air out of clothing, thus enabling me to cram in a greater volume of souvenirs. The agent in Osaka, where even checked baggage is screened, found my squashed laundry fascinating. She methodically removed each bag and undid the zip lock to reinflate the contents. She seemed to delight in rummaging through my dirty underwear piece by piece, before replacing each one precisely where I'd had it and resealing the bags.

She then squeezed the air out and replaced the bags in the suitcase before turning her attention to my toilet kit. At the delicate point when the agent was separating the bristles on my toothbrush, one of my traveling companions, in a loud voice, opined that I must look like a terrorist. Thank all the Buddhist, Shinto and Christian gods, the security agent didn't understand her English, thus saving us from being dragged off to jail for in-depth questioning.

Most people would agree that I do not fit the profile of an Al Qaeda member. I suspect that for every Middle Eastern-looking young man, an unlucky old lady is searched. I trust you will sleep better tonight knowing that the agent confiscated my infant-size nail clippers before allowing me to proceed to the plane.

I must tell you that these experiences felt a lot more comfortable than the last time I found myself across a desk from a customs agent.

In 1947, heading for a flight from Hungary to Switzerland, when I was 10 years old and traveling alone, I carried Eureka, my teddy bear, under my arm. I was being shipped out of the country under the pretext of a Red Cross-sponsored holiday, in an attempt by my family to flee the Russian occupation.

My small brown cardboard suitcase had already been cleared by the Russian customs agent when a mean-looking, tall, overweight security officer behind the counter called after me. His harsh features and sardonic smile sent shivers down my young spine. He stared at me as he demanded to see my bear. I handed my gold-furred bruin over to him. He turned the 9-inch beast every which way, tugging at its fur, inspecting its beady eyes and ear cavities.

While holding Eureka in his large, sweaty palm, the Russian Army uniformed agent peered over the counter and looked me up and down. His glance stopped and was riveted on my feet. Without looking, I knew what he was glaring at. I had worn one red sock and one green and white striped, on purpose that morning, to create a conversation piece. Together these colors represented the Hungarian flag.

"Your socks don't match," the agent informed me in broken Hungarian.

I studied my feet for a minute before replying, "Patriotic though, don't you think?"

It occurred to me that I should have worn a pair with the hammer and sickle on it. The agent let out a judgmental grunt and extended the bear toward me. As I reached for my prize possession, he felt its weight.

"Why is this bear so heavy?" he asked. "What's in it, young lady?" the agent demanded. Though he gave me the creeps and I was frightened, I tried to keep my voice steady.

"Sawdust, I would imagine," I replied. In those days stuffed animals often contained sawdust. Having observed my father deal with petty bureaucrats in his job as a museum director, I tried to copy his air of authority and added with some bravado: "Just slit him open, if you don't believe me. It will make a proper mess."

He fixed his eyes on me again and I gave him my most innocent gaze. He mopped his forehead with a dirty handkerchief and handed Eureka back to me.

I tucked the bear back under my arm, picked up my little suitcase, turned and headed for the gate. My mother stood behind a rope, cordoned off from the departing passengers. I looked over at her, winked and gave her a smile. Nestled in the belly of my beast were 10 gold Krugerrands.

My mother eventually managed to cross the Iron Curtain to join me and in 1949 we emigrated to America. Those gold coins constituted our entire fortune when we arrived in the United States.

Confessions
of a
Court
Commissioner

*Our current mayor will be relieved to know
that the following arrived at my desk long
before he took office. However, the sentiments
expressed could have been written yesterday.
I've left the spelling for you to enjoy:*

"Dears:

Ten dollars probley ain't much to you!

Your Mayor stinks! It's to bad your city
takes care of its none workers & fines
the people who care. St. Francis would
turn in His grave, if He knew how uncar-
ing the politicians have become over the
working mans rights.

Doesn't seem it pays to be responsible!
Just be a welfare bum and you get every
thing.

I'm old, upset and sick of being a goat for
the lazy politicians who sit on their fat
behinds and do nothing but draw their
fat pay checks."

ROACHES, ROACHES EVERYWHERE

A cockroach drowned in a puddle of urine at the Hall of Justice. Is that cruel and unusual punishment?

The critters used to be a part of everyday life at the Hall. They must have chomped their way through the last piece of toast before the cafeteria closed for remodeling. However, roaches still presided over illegal hot plates, toaster ovens and other paraphernalia, throughout the building.

Now that I am retired, cockroaches scurry through memories of my days in court.

Leroy claimed the roaches gained weight faster than he did, no matter how many donuts he consumed.

Leroy was once one of the public defenders' regular clients, who seemed to live in the corridor, outside their offices and my courtroom, at the Hall of Justice. No one knew where he spent his nights when the building closed. The P.D.s fed and clothed Leroy and generally looked out for his welfare when he was not in jail. A sweet and gentle man, he gained their sympathies because he had a saucer-shaped dent on the side of his head. He'd had a late-night encounter with a mugger sometime in the past. Leroy looked oddly comical as a result. He suffered from a slight mental defect — not enough to keep him out of the criminal justice system, but enough to make him unable to function in the harsh world outside.

Leroy was a rumpled little fellow, weighing perhaps 110 pounds. His crinkled face offered a lopsided, impish grin to all who passed by the bench where he presided. He had sad, basset-hound eyes and closely cropped gray hair. Most of the time, a bowler hat perched at a cocky angle on top of his head to hide the dent. When he sat, he'd lean forward, both hands and chin resting on a cane, á la Charlie Chaplin, whom Leroy admired. He kept his worldly goods stashed under his feet, tied in a modest bundle, in imitation of his idol.

Leroy ate constantly. He loved sugar donuts from the deli across Bryant Street, but declined all offerings from the cafeteria. It became a standing joke around the Hall of Justice that you'd best not bring Leroy anything from the House of Toast in the basement, because his tastes had evolved far beyond that in-house fare.

"Their roaches are too crunchy," he'd say.

Leroy may have been somewhat dim-witted due to his head injury, but he knew enough to play the system just right. Each year as winter approached, he'd break into a car or commit some other misdemeanor, just severe enough to get him sentenced to jail, so he could spend the rainy season as a guest of the sheriff. He thus avoided sleeping on the streets in inclement weather. One year, a neophyte public defender, not understanding the game plan, put up a rigorous defense on Leroy's behalf. As a result, the judge assigned Leroy to SWAP, the Sheriff's Work Alternative Program, rather than to jail. Saturday would be his first day on trash pickup detail.

The next morning, Leroy and I exchanged good mornings. "Work ain't for the likes of me, Judge," he muttered, visibly upset, pointing at the dent on the side of his head.

"Tough luck, eh, Leroy?" I replied as I followed my bailiff through the side door into the courtroom. She relocked the door behind us.

Traffic court was staffed for security by the police department, not the sheriff's office. My protector Lisa, was a Chinese-American officer, who stood 4 feet 11 inches in her stocking feet and handled her duties with brains rather than brawn.

Most days, Leroy wandered in and out of courtrooms, observing his public defender friends in action. Though in traffic court there were no public defenders (the people appearing in pro per, i.e., without attorneys), Leroy still spent considerable time sitting in the back row. It wasn't until he started muttering to himself that I realized why he paid us these visits.

The day after he had been sentenced to work for the sheriff, Leroy sauntered into court as soon as Officer Lisa unlocked the door. He took up his accustomed seat and started mumbling. The noise attracted Lisa's attention, and she rose from her perch near the front of the courtroom, walked toward Leroy and admonished him to be quiet. After a few minutes, the muttering resumed. When Lisa stood up again and approached Leroy, he gave her a little smile and quieted down. Lisa returned to her seat, only to have to get up again moments later.

The longer I observed this minuet between my petite guardian and the equally diminutive Leroy, the clearer it became that he relished the encounters and thrived on Lisa's attention. Lisa had allowed him to take a few impromptu dance steps with her at the annual Christmas party a few days prior to his sentencing hearing. It became apparent that Leroy had grown quite fond of my bailiff. The rest of the week, he spent part of every day just hanging around, gazing at her.

Officer Lisa, though appearing small and helpless, in fact had passed the police department's rigorous physical with flying colors. Defendants and court watchers alike were tempted to test her, Leroy being no exception. When she lost her patience, she would order him out of the courtroom. Depending on his mood, he'd either rise with a sigh and shuffle out the door or hold his ground.

On Friday, when I handed a cup of coffee to Leroy at his usual place in the hallway, he gave me a rakish grin, his wrinkled old face lighting up. I asked him, "What are you so happy about?"

"She loves me," came the instant reply, while he nodded toward Lisa, who stood nearby, unlocking the courtroom door. Lisa's head snapped around when she heard Leroy's remark. She glared at him, looked at me, and rolled her eyes toward heaven.

No sooner had I called the first case on the morning calendar, than into the courtroom walked Leroy, coffee cup in hand. He knew Officer Lisa would come to tell him to take the coffee outside, and she did not disappoint him. Leroy bowed in her direction and, with a wicked grin, slurped the last of his coffee and chucked the empty cup in the wastebasket near the door. I soon became engrossed in my work and only once in a while took note of Leroy, who sat in the back row, quiet as a mouse, gazing at Lisa for the rest of the morning. She studiously ignored him, complaining to me at recess that she wished he would cut it out.

Leroy reappeared promptly at 1:30, for the afternoon calendar. Returning from lunch, as I walked through the courtroom to go to my chambers, I could hear him start to whistle quietly and noted a corresponding bristle from Lisa. Not an auspicious start to Leroy's afternoon.

When I took the bench, I noticed that Leroy had quieted and sat holding one hand behind his back, smiling at Lisa. During the third case I called, the defendant, who had been cited for plugging up an intersection, tried to convince me that he thought it safer to drive through on a stale yellow light, than to stop. Leroy began to hum at a level too loud to ignore. Strains of "Mona Lisa" wafted through the courtroom, distracting the defendant, who turned to look at him and lost his train of thought.

Officer Lisa, blushing crimson, leapt to her feet, kicking over the wastebasket in her haste. Roaches, caught mid-snack, scurried for cover. A woman sitting in the front row let out a squeal. All eyes turned in Lisa's direction. Ignoring the woman, Lisa pulled herself up to her full 4 foot 11 and headed for the back of the courtroom, crunching roaches under her shoes with every step. Leroy watched her approach and just before she reached him, he pulled a single red rose from behind his back. He extended his arm in Lisa's direction, much to the amusement of those of us watching.

Without breaking her stride, ignoring the offered blossom, she grabbed Leroy by the collar of his jacket, at the scruff of his neck. She lifted him from his chair as though he were a feather and held him just inches above the ground, leaving

Leroy dangling like a puppet. In the blur of a few seconds, Leroy managed to stick the stem of the rose between his teeth, form an enigmatic smile, flail his arms and legs á la Charlie Chaplin and keep right on humming "Mona Lisa," never missing a beat. Officer Lisa opened the swinging doors with her hip and ejected Leroy from the courtroom. On his way out, Leroy gave us his best impish grin and tipped his bowler in a farewell salute.

There was no maintaining judicial decorum that time.

"To Whomever May Unconcern:

Please find enclosed $20 for
attached parking ticket,
although I could swear that
that fire hydrant creeped
up and planted itself next to
my car."

I DREAMED I KISSED YOUR HAND, MADAME

When I worked as night duty commissioner, my dreams often blended with phone conversations I'd had with the police. It seemed to me that even when I worked days, I had a vivid nightlife.

Once I dreamed that I — not Ted Kaczynski — was the Unabomber. In my dream, I kept lifting manhole covers, dropping into strange and dirty places below the street. I waded through tunnels, sloshing through stinking, stagnant water, kicking aside rats swimming at my heels. I climbed up to lift the next manhole cover, and peered up and down the street. Sheriff's deputies lined the boulevard and pointed at me, shouting for me to give myself up. I pulled the cover back into place and scrambled down again.

It seems to me this dream might have been sponsored by a burrito I had eaten the night before.

Me the Unabomber? That's a laugh. Tell that to the strange man who tried to catch me doing something illegal or at least something immoral. I was alerted to his shadowing me by Ann Wren, a private eye he tried to hire when his own efforts had failed.

"We didn't take the job," she informed me. "Just thought you might want to check him out, though I think he's harmless. His name is Henry Hawkins, and he's been tailing you for two years now. He knows all about you from your neighbors, Judge. Where you live, your children's names, where you volunteer — all sorts of stuff. He said he didn't like the ruling you made against his wife in small claims court. He wanted us to find something on you, so he could get you fired."

From the address the private eye had given me, I realized that Mr. Hawkins lived down the block from a place where I volunteered. The Fry Center housed non-violent female offenders and their children under age two. I went there every week for board meetings and to give respite to the mothers by playing with the children. The thought that Mr. Hawkins had been stalking me left me feeling uneasy. As it happened, my friend Police Captain Matt Downing lived on the same block as Mr. Hawkins. I told Matt about the phone call from Ann Wren and asked if he could informally drop by his neighbor's house to see what he could learn.

Matt reported to me the next day. "You won't believe this, but Henry Hawkins is a retired San Francisco State University professor. The detective was right. He's harmless. Hawkins worked himself into a lather two years ago, and once he started on his mission to have you fired, Hawkins just couldn't let go. I told him he was lucky you didn't have him arrested and to knock off the surveillance. Professor Hawkins stepped outside with me when I was leaving, so his wife couldn't hear, and muttered an embarrassed apology. I don't think he'll give you any more trouble," Matt said.

Good thing Hawkins didn't follow me into my dreams!

❋   ❋   ❋

Before parking citations were removed from the jurisdiction of the court, I listened day after day to people's parking travails. Towed cars and damaged vehicles figured prominently in my days.

One night, I dreamed that the other traffic referee employed by the court and I were sitting in a car on top of an elevator. A giant scooping mechanism reached in and slowly flipped the vehicle backward, hurling us into the shaft.

Wouldn't the parking protesters have loved to see that?

●　　●　　●

After a particularly raucous session in child support court, where an alleged father was confronted by four mothers — all braless — charging him with paternity, I went home and dreamed that I had lost control of the courtroom. I hadn't read the case files, couldn't find the day's calendar. My children were toddlers again, climbing on the windowsill in the courtroom, avoiding my best efforts to catch them. My bailiff signaled to me that he had to go to his second job and couldn't stay another minute, then exited the courtroom.

My clerks, who sat below my podium and to the front of me, were engrossed in playing solitaire on their computers and, no matter how I tried (including throwing spitballs at their heads), I couldn't get their attention. Several people were smoking pot in the back of the courtroom, while an African-American Boy Scout troop visiting the courts on a field trip, came through the double doors, wide-eyed at the confusion. Their leader gave me a dirty look and said, "Who's in charge here? And why aren't you wearing a bra?"

In the midst of this nightmare, I was awakened by a telephone call from a police officer. After issuing an emergency protective order, I went back to sleep, and the dream continued. I found myself riding in the back of a Goodwill truck with an open tailgate. I rummaged through donated merchandise, desperately looking for a bra. When I located one, I saw pedestrians glaring at me from the sidewalk. All of them seemed to have been in my court at one time or another. I wanted to pull off my shirt to put on the bra without anyone noticing. Just as I decided the time was right, a defendant who had been in court that morning leered at me from the window of a passing car.

●　　●　　●

Bus drivers were frequent defendants in traffic court. Is it any wonder that my sympathies for their travails increased after I dreamed that I was one? In the dream, all the passengers were wearing 4-inch heels and were busily squashing cockroaches in the aisle. I tried to steer through traffic on Mission Street, while a chihuahua-size roach lodged itself between the gas pedal and the floor. A sweet young thing climbed onto the front fender of the bus I was driving across 16th Street, turned her back to me, and spread her arms over the windshield as if the bus were the Titanic. "Bring on DiCaprio!" she yelled.

＊　＊　＊

A few days after I had dismissed a minor traffic infraction citation for a German tourist, I met him in the courthouse elevator.

"I dreamed I kissed your hand, Madame," the man told me, quoting a translation of an old song I happened to have learned from German soldiers during World War II.

Into my brain popped the refrain from my early childhood: "Because I cannot stand your face." I gave him a knowing smile and — as the elevator doors opened and he stepped out — wondered what the proper judicial response to his remark should have been.

THE TRUTH OR NOT THE TRUTH

At the approach to the Golden Gate Bridge, a bright yellow sign directs bicyclists to use the east sidewalk on weekdays and the west sidewalk on weekends. Since I'm often alone on the bridge on Sundays at dawn, I ignore the directive and pedal my bike across on the east side, where the view of the sunrise is more spectacular.

Is this a moving violation? I mused on a recent morning while committing this heinous crime. The sunrise defense wouldn't fly, even in my court.

I pass the pole with the Suicide Prevention hotline phone attached, remembering my days as a volunteer for that organization.

A lone jogger running toward me rounds the south tower. She and I are the only two people on the east sidewalk. She strides with dogged determination and, as the gap between us narrows, I ride to the far right, giving her three-quarters of the pavement on which to pass. While she is still some 30 feet away, she begins gesturing, jerking her right arm in the direction of the west sidewalk. Her red nylon shorts cling to her legs, and her white T-shirt is stained with perspiration.

She continues to gesticulate. I know she's telling me that I belong on the west sidewalk. Since I can't very well cross the six lanes of traffic to accommodate her, I open my mouth to form the word "sorry," as she approaches.

She makes an abrupt move into my path and stops, her face contorted with fury. I swerve, barely missing her and the 1-foot concrete ledge that separates the sidewalk from car traffic.

"I'm patrolling for Suicide Prevention. Do you need any help?" comes out of my mouth, unbidden. Helping her over the side and into the drink is what I have in mind.

"Oh, I'm so sorry," sputters my antagonist, her eyes opening wide to take in my official-looking yellow windbreaker, with the Golden Gate National Recreation Area patch on the sleeve.

"It's all right. People who ride on the wrong side are annoying," I respond, words laden with syrup. I resume my bike ride, chuckling all the way to Sausalito.

Traffic has increased on the Golden Gate by the time I head back to San Francisco, and I ride demurely on the west sidewalk, where I belong.

I can't help but think about all the petty lawbreakers, many of whom blurted out minor untruths when they appeared before me in traffic court. Who was I to judge them?

There was no deputy district attorney assigned to my court. When the recipient of a moving violation wanted to contest the validity of the charge, the police officer who issued the ticket came to court and told his version of what had happened. Hope springs eternal in the hearts of traffic violators. If the officer failed to show up at the appointed time, the ticket was dismissed. When luck ran out and the officer in fact appeared, creative genius often took over.

One morning in court, Officer Maguire described observing the defendant run a blinking red light, without making any effort to slow down, let alone come to a stop at the intersection of 18th Avenue and Fulton Streets.

The defendant, Charles Chan, who resembled his movie-fame namesake, stood before me and gave me a beatific smile. He declared, "But Your Honor, I went through on the blink."

Then Mr. Chan erased the smile on his face and proclaimed, "I rest my case."

Another defendant, Hilda Neustadt, clutched her California driver's license in her hand while she spoke to me in English with a heavy German accent. She did not deny having run a stop sign. Instead, she tried to convince me to dismiss her citation, claiming that she could not read the sign because of her limited English.

From the corner of my eye, I saw Officer Nuñez roll his eyes toward heaven, though he remained silent.

"How did you get your driver's license if you can't read English, Ms. Neustadt?" I asked, pointing toward the one she held in her hand.

"Friend took test," she declared.

"The truth, the whole truth and nothing but the truth, Judge," pronounced Officer Nuñez, as I bit my lip to keep from laughing.

"Your Worship: I write to beg your pardon. I'm visiting from England and got two tickets, two days in a row, for not curbing my wheels. When I received the first one, I could not decide what I had done wrong. I parked on 18th Street, by Church. Next day I got another one for the same thing at 18th and Castro. My American friend told me there is a law that I must curb my wheels on a hill. Begging your pardon, but I didn't think either location was the slightest hilly.

I promise you, from now on, my wheels will have more curves than Bo Derek!"

(I mustn't let the salutation go to my head!)

CONVENT GIRLS IN THE CLOSET

"Keep your hands to yourself," warned one of the nuns, when she saw me pat my classmate on the back, congratulating her on making a basketball shot.

"Hands to yourself," and eventually the word "hands," was enough to remind us convent girls that evil lurked in getting too familiar with classmates of the same sex. Fifty years later, many of us are still uneasy about being touched — let alone hugged — by a female friend.

Classmates from convent school who were, in fact, gay stayed deep in the closet for many years. Those who had gay offspring termed their children's partners "roommates."

The thousands of same-sex weddings that took place at San Francisco's City Hall until they were halted by the California Supreme Court a month later, caused ripples far beyond the gay community. It's not just a political battle that is raging, not just a civil rights issue being fought. On a much more personal level, lots of people are affected and are seeking liberation in so many ways. Even among the Convent of the Sacred Heart, Menlo Park, Class of '54, emails with attachments of wedding pictures marking the marriages of gay children were circulated.

In my role as a retired court commissioner, I was asked by Kay, the daughter of a convent friend, to officiate at her wedding. Though her mother, Helen, and I have been good friends for 54 years, and Kay has been aware she is a lesbian for the past 20 years, Helen only told me a couple of years ago that Kay is gay.

City Hall was bedecked with flowers in mid-February 2004 for nearly 4,000 weddings. I could feel palpable joy as soon as I entered the building. Bouquets, garlands, boutonnieres abounded, red roses predominated. A half-dozen marriage ceremonies were going on at various points on the grand staircase under the ornate dome. My husband, Irwin, and I met Kay and her partner, Leslie at the county clerk's office, where the two women would pick up their marriage license.

Irwin wanted to attend the ceremony to leave no doubt in our young friends' minds that he supported their marriage. Helen waited for us with Kim, the two-year-old daughter of Kay and Leslie. While the two brides stood in line, we sat and watched the parade of happy couples picking up their paperwork. A young man and woman walked by, holding hands, looking out of place. An ironic twist for this straight couple caught up in the midst of the history-making gay marriages.

As Kay and Leslie stood in line at the marriage license counter, a stranger approached them, handing Leslie a gorgeous bouquet of yellow, pink, white and red tulips. "Congratulations," the man said. "These came from anonymous well-wishers in New Zealand. Flowers have been pouring in from all over the world," he smiled before disappearing into the crowd of family and friends of the many couples waiting to be married. Tears welled in Leslie's eyes.

What other recent event had caused such an outpouring of affection? None that I can recall. There was global horror at the events of 9/11 and international sadness at the death of Princess Diana, but a worldwide circle of joy? Even the Libertarian Party had a member handing out red roses to each participant.

I'd dressed meticulously before leaving home, putting on nylons, a creamy silk blouse and a skirt, to make sure that I properly represented the judiciary. I donned my judicial robe as our wedding party walked from the clerk's office to the great hall under the rotunda, creating a properly solemn figure. We climbed the grand staircase and found the best camera angle so Helen could record the big event.

Kay and Leslie were both teary-eyed by the time I intoned " ... so long as you both shall live?" Their yeses came laden with emotion and with smiles of love for each other.

As the two women, their little daughter linking hands with them, descended the beautiful stairway, those gathered for similar ceremonies all over the grand hall erupted in applause. The sound of their clapping reverberated from the cupola, making it seem as though thousands were cheering.

Perhaps it was just my imagination, but as I looked at the broad smiles on Kay and Leslie's faces and at the delighted child being led down the stairs by her mothers, I thought I heard a collective sigh of relief from all those long ago convent girls.

"Dear Distinguished Lady of
the Court,

Even though you fined me ten
dollars, I still think you're a fair
and honest law-decider. (You
even say "you're welcome" after
someone says thank you.) And
I do believe you can see right
through the ones who are hiding
the truth.

But the motorcycle cops should
have something better to do at
five in the morning ... Oh, well ...

Thank you for listening to a
disturbed (not deranged, yet)
citizen."

STARS ABOVE THE NAKED CITY

My volunteering at San Francisco General Hospital's nursery provided an extra pair of hands for the overworked nurses, and some added human contact, in the midst of high-tech care for the babies. It also served as an antidote to my new post as family law commissioner. During that assignment, I spent my days trying, and often failing, to bring order out of the chaos in people's lives.

For a short while each week before family tragedies engulfed me, I escaped into the world of infants. Though the lives of their parents may have been royally screwed up, it was not for me to do anything about them, and I sensed in the babies, infinite possibilities.

One particular Tuesday, dawn had not yet broken as I crossed the parking lot and entered the hospital. An old line from a television show ran through my head: "There are so many stories in the naked city."

I got a hint of those stories every time I made my way through the emergency department, the only unlocked entrance at 4:30 in the morning, when my shift started. Dawn hours fit well with my insomnia and gave a boost to my difficult working day, which began at the courthouse at nine.

I yawned as I picked my way among the sleeping bodies lying on the floor of the emergency room, oblivious to the fluorescent lights and noise around them. These were people who had trumped up ailments to get off the street for the night.

An ambulance crew wheeled in a gurney bearing a gunshot victim already hooked up to IVs, giving him life support. The attendants also made their way between the sleeping figures on the floor.

The first glimpse of my charges came through the glass wall, which exposed the neonatal nursery to the sixth-floor corridor. The babies, swaddled like little Eskimos in pastel-colored blankets, each lay in a clear plastic bassinet. The dimmed lights created an atmosphere of quiet calm.

For the first of many scrubbings of the morning, I used the disinfectant soap at the sinks across the hall from the nursery and donned a sterile gown. I was ready to enter the world of tomorrow.

Helen, the nurse in charge, whose furrowed brow gave her a stern outward appearance worthy of Nurse Ratched, greeted me with her usual crisp, "Good morning." Volunteering under her direction, I'd learned that her severe exterior covered a marshmallow heart.

"Come meet Mitsuko," she said, leading the way to one of the bassinets. "She's a 4-pounder. Her mom's tiny, too," she explained, picking up Mitsuko with the utmost care and handing her to me. The baby's tiny butt fit into the palm of my hand. I sat down in one of the rocking chairs scattered throughout the nursery and felt the warmth emanating from Mitsuko's body as I began to rock her. Helen tended another baby while telling me Mitsuko's story.

"Her mama is studying at San Francisco State as an exchange student and became pregnant by a man who promised to marry her. He strung her along for seven months before she found out he's already married. According to Japanese custom, her parents disowned her, so she can't go home. She's hoping to keep the baby and make a life for herself. She's applied for permanent residence in the U.S., but doesn't know if she'll get it," Helen concluded.

Mitsuko's features were smooth and angular, revealing her high cheekbones. She had inch-long jet-black hair, which glistened under the light shining on her from a neighboring heat lamp. She exuded an air of physical well-being.

"She's a bit of a pig," Helen said as she handed me a 4-ounce bottle of breast milk, which was dropped off by Mitsuko's mom the night before. Mom was discharged a couple of days before, but the baby needed to gain a bit more weight before she could join her. Mitsuko sucked her bottle with gusto, pausing only to give me a gas-induced smile.

I hoped her mom could stay in America. This kid would make a sturdy little citizen.

The nurses were expecting a new arrival from the delivery room across the hall. A smiling boy, about 10, soon appeared at the nursery door, carrying a bundled-up infant.

"I'm Roberto, and this is my brother Francisco," he announced for all of us to hear. "He weighs 8 pounds, 10 ounces. And that's my brother Luis," the boy tossed his head in the direction of a child walking next to him. Roberto held the baby with two hands out in front of his body, elbows resting on his hips, as though he were carrying frankincense to the Baby Jesus. Roberto and Luis, having been present at the birth, were both dressed in the green-and-white-striped sterile gowns worn by volunteers. The gowns reached the floor on both boys, making walking somewhat perilous. Their proud papa, smiling from ear to ear, walked right behind Roberto, watching his every step. Through the glass wall I saw the mom being wheeled on a gurney toward the maternity ward. She gave a tired smile and waved to her children.

I stroked Mitsuko's head after laying her in her bassinet and went in search for a couple of sterile shirts of the kind worn by doctors.

"Try these on," I suggested to the two boys when I returned. Roberto deposited the newborn into a bassinet under a heat lamp, as directed by Nurse Helen. The two brothers wiggled into the shirts, which reached to their knees, less likely to trip them.

"Now you are doctors," I told them, and they beamed at me.

"Gracias, señora," Roberto said.

"Let's go get some breakfast, boys," their father suggested, the stress of the last few hours reflecting on his face. "We'll be back in a little bit." The brothers took their dad's hands and marched with him from the nursery.

Tom, a lab technician the size and color of Muhammad Ali, appeared and ever so gently attached an IV to the infant's arm, using some clear plastic to hold the IV in place. I noticed that Francisco is a bit jaundiced. His skin wrinkled up under the tape. Francisco's pale pink hand looked like a rose petal, enveloped in Tom's giant palm.

I returned to check on Mitsuko. She was half the size of Francisco, but perfect in her own way. Her lips were making sucking movements as she slept.

Next to Mitsuko, in another plastic bassinet, lay little Woody Taylor. He had been in the nursery for several weeks. Woody was Baby "A" of a pair of twins. Baby "B" died two days after the boys' premature birth. Woody hung on, though he wasn't thriving. Since his mom was on methadone, Woody had to be weaned from his inherited addiction. He whimpered as his frail little body had spasms. I reached to rub his back, but he continued to fidget.

When my twin granddaughters, Eva and Sarah, were infants, they had shared a crib. They would wiggle around, agitated, until they managed to touch each other. The closer they lay, the better they liked it.

I wonder whether Woody missed Baby B whose body he had been entangled with for nine months, so I cup his face in my hands. I could feel his facial muscles relax as he quieted and resumed rhythmic breathing. I stood for a long time, looking at Woody's features, while I continued to hold his face. The shape of Woody's head resembled that of a mouse. I smoothed his brow and stroked his neck, trying to touch every exposed part of him. His skin felt like fine silk under my hands. As I turned Woody onto his side, I wondered if he'd miss his twin all his life. For now, he slept.

I noticed that Abdul is sitting in his usual place at the far corner of the nursery. The father of a heroin baby, Abdul had been coming every evening after work, spending the night sitting with his infant daughter. The week before, he told me he had divorced the baby's mother because she wouldn't stop using drugs no matter how he begged her. They hadn't known she was pregnant.

"I'm taking Jasmine to Morocco when she hits 5 pounds," he told me, after I said good morning. "She's up to 4 pounds, 3 ounces," he announced with pride.

He glanced out the window behind him, looking at the sky. The last of the night's stars held its own against the rising sun.

"I wish I could take all these babies," Abdul remarked, "and lift them to the sky where there is no pain and leave them there, suspended in the heavens."

His eloquence touched me and I draped my arm around his shoulders and hugged him. It was time for me to retrace my steps, to leave the stars behind for another week and head for the courthouse.

There was something endearing about those who struggle with English:

"Hy Dear: Officer:

I have the language problems.
Thus I write down my protest for
my violent ticket. A plain police
thought I was stock the traffic
on Grant Ave. Actually, it was
to crowed, many cars in front of
mine, I couldn't move my car,
and the police didn't listen to
my explain. He just wrote down
a violate ticket and left it on my
windshield. So that I wish you
could give me a good judgment,
just because I wasn't on purpose to
stock the traffic road.

Yours truly."

THE LITTLE REDHEADED BOY

He stood at the defendant's counsel table in Judge Cartwright's court, fresh out of law school. If he had been wearing shorts and a T-shirt instead of a brown, ill-fitting suit, he could have been in kindergarten, he looked so young. Freckles covered the bridge of his pug nose, and his head sprouted flaming red ringlets. That first day, I dubbed him "The Little Redheaded Boy," and thoughts of him have always made me smile.

I, too, was fresh out of law school at the time, working for his opponent, Edith Pierce, who represented the plaintiff. Edith, the barracuda of lady lawyers, made a daily habit of chewing up and spitting out young attorneys. She had just made her grand entrance into the courtroom, timed to coincide with Judge Cartwright's taking the bench. I had been sent ahead to save the center front seat for her, so that she could fling her full-length mink on the chair for dramatic effect, while her eyes swept opposing counsel with a look of contempt. All eyes would then be riveted on her as she made eye contact with the judge and said, "Good morning, Your Honor," in a voice laden with respectful familiarity.

The Little Redheaded Boy appeared on behalf of the defendant, to represent him in a prominent divorce case. He had filed a Motion for Continuance, to gain time to gather information and respond to a particularly oppressive batch of interrogatories Edith had served on his client. Any other lawyer would have stipulated to the continuance and there was no question but that the judge would grant it. Edith, however, never stipulated to anything, thus necessitating the young attorney's appearance.

Judge Cartwright called the case, and The Little Redheaded Boy flushed when he identified himself as representing the defendant.

"We submit on the pleadings, Your Honor," he managed to squeak at a pubescent octave.

"Hrumph," grunted Mrs. Pierce. "Your Honor, if it please the Court ..."

"It does not, Counsel," interrupted Judge Cartwright, mindful of his lengthy calendar and Mrs. Pierce's proclivity toward dramatic presentations. "I've read the pleadings. Defendant's motion is granted. Will you prepare the order for my signature and serve it on opposing counsel, Mrs. Pierce?" said the judge, reaching for the next file.

"It was defendant's motion, Your Honor, but if the court pleases, I'll prepare the order and serve it. Provided, of course, that counsel for defendant has an address." She looked across the room at opposing counsel with utter disdain.

The blush rose by degrees from The Little Redheaded Boy's collar, up his neck to his chin, and worked its way around, enveloping his freckled face.

Dear God, I thought, squirming with discomfort at her insult to a fellow neophyte, let him have an office and not be working out of some apartment in a dingy neighborhood.

The Little Redheaded Boy pulled in his stomach and puffed out his chest. "300 Montgomery Street, Your Honor," he said.

Several veteran attorneys in attendance couldn't help but clap at his recitation of what proved to be such a respectable address. The judge frowned at this outburst.

Mrs. Pierce harrumphed again, passed her file to me and swept up her mink on her way out of the courtroom. Her opponent looked as though he had been through the wringer, but smiled nervously as he followed her out.

Fifteen years later, that young attorney had become one of the army of inter-changeable deputy district attorneys. He was deep in negotiation with a public defender outside a courtroom at the Hall of Justice when I spotted him. I had been appointed a traffic referee and worked in the same building. He had tamed his red curls into a crew cut worthy of an FBI agent and donned the pinstriped navy blue uniform favored by D.A.s. He appeared to be brimming with self-confidence. Rumor had it that even Edith Pierce was in awe of his prosecutorial powers. I liked him better in his prior incarnation.

Another five years passed. I saw him dashing out of the rain into a Starbucks. He now looked distinguished in his Burberry coat, but not even the raindrops running down his head could eradicate the worry lines on his face, nor the gray around his temples. Some people should remain forever young. Though we have never met, his aging brought home to me my own mortality. In my mind, he is frozen in time the way he looked twenty years ago. I longed to see The Little Red-headed Boy once again.

"I was sitting in the park on the grass, a few dogs running and playing nearby. A small one sat behind me and belonged to a person I had met before.

A police officer walked up and asked if it was mine. I said no, but I would be willing to hold onto her leash until her dad came back. The officer asked if I would claim responsibility for the dog. I said no; that it was not mine. The officer then picked up the dog's leash and said he was going to take her away. I begged him not to because I knew the dog's father didn't have enough money to get her out of the pound (he is unemployed and his wife is pregnant). The officer said I would have to take responsibility, so I agreed and he began to write me a ticket.

If this ticket is undisputable, I will understand. Being taken to the pound is very traumatic for an animal, especially a dog, because dogs are so attached to their families. I couldn't let that dog feel abandoned, alone and smell fear and death. Please try to understand."

(And that's just what I tried to do!)

THE GHOST RIDER

The old rusty freighter, loaded with containers, sounded its horn as it passed under the Golden Gate Bridge. I saw its name, Obake Noruhito, across its bow as I pedaled from San Francisco to Marin at sunrise. Curious about the Japanese name, I later asked a friend to translate. She told me that the closest she could come to it in English would be "The Ghost Rider."

As I continued on, winding my way down the bike path toward Fort Baker, a cyclist was heading the opposite way on the 12 percent grade. As we passed each other, I saw his sinewy muscles straining to make the hill. He gave me a cheery "Good morning" as we passed, and I noticed that he was very old. His face, wrinkled by time, appeared chiseled, and from under his helmet a shock of gray hair protruded, emphasizing his steel-blue eyes. His smile indicated that he was at peace with the world, and his greeting cheered me. Fewer and fewer riders bother to say hello to me; sometimes I think I am becoming invisible, as my own hair turns gray, and the age gap widens between most riders and me.

After breakfast in Sausalito, I headed back toward the bridge and home. Halfway up the hill I noticed the same old man, again pedaling toward the crest.

"Where are you headed?" I asked as I pulled alongside.

"I am going up and down the hill to train for a trip across the Pyrenees in the spring," he replied.

"I have trouble getting up the hill just once in a day, let alone going up and down it for hours," I said with admiration.

"It's simple," he said. "Never look up to see how much farther you have to go, and put out of your mind any idea that you can get off." He paused, "Besides, it's the journey that counts."

We rode together to the top and he told me he was 82 and had been riding bikes all his life. I wished him luck on his upcoming trip, and his eyes sparkled as he wheeled around to go back down the hill and start again.

The old man rode with me now and then in my imagination. I found hills easier to pedal when I didn't look up or think about getting off. Most of all, I just enjoyed the journeys. I wondered if he had made it across the Pyrenees.

Three years later, I saw him again. He was lying on his back on the pavement, close to the top of the hill, on the same path where we had met. A Highway Patrol car shielded his body, and a couple of people had stopped to help. The old man was lying still, his eyes closed. There was a smile on his face. I did not stop to ask what had happened because it came to me with absolute certainty that his journey had come to an end.

Is there a special heaven for bikers? If so, I hope to go there someday because for sure the old man is there. If there is no such place, I hope he was headed downhill, enjoying the ride, when he died.

As I rode onto the bridge, a blanket of fog rolled through the Golden Gate. A foghorn sounded its mournful lament. The mists swirled just over the surface of the bay and the outline of a ship appeared. I could barely make out the words "Obake Noruhito" on its hull before the fog enveloped The Ghost Rider once again.

MY MONGOLIAN ANCESTORS

It all started as a joke, more out of boredom than serious intent. Back in 1973, I was procrastinating in my law school's library, putting off reading the assigned case law by browsing through the New York Times. A short item caught my eye:

> Minority Women Being Recruited by State Department.
>
> The State Department has announced that minority women will be admitted to serve in the Foreign Service on oral examination, without taking the written exam.

It had been my life's ambition to become a Foreign Service officer, before I was sidetracked by love and marriage. Ten years and four children later, when my marriage began to falter, I took the Foreign Service exam in the hope of providing myself with a way to make a living. I flunked the economics portion of the exam and decided to pursue a career in law instead.

When I saw the notice, I facetiously dashed off a note to the State Department:

> "Gentlemen: I am a Hungarian immigrant. Hungary was invaded by the Mongols in the 13th century. It is likely, therefore, that although I am blue eyed and fair, I have some Mongolian ancestry. I wish, therefore, to apply to be admitted to the Foreign Service under your new guidelines for minorities."

It never occurred to me that they would take me seriously. However, by return mail, I received a request for proof of minority ancestry and failing that, urged me to apply for the written examination. Joke over, I thought nothing more about it. A couple of years went by before I received an inquiry from a New York law firm. Having obtained a list of minority applicants from the State Department, they wanted to know whether I was interested in participating in a class action lawsuit, based on the notion that the State Department did not ask African-Americans to prove that they are African-American, nor the Chinese to prove that they are Chinese and, therefore, could not ask me to prove that I was Mongolian.

Although by this time I was practicing law, I could not resist taking part in this very American adventure — a class action suit.

Again, a couple of years passed without further communication from the New York avenging angels. Eight years after I had answered the original ad and the class action suit had wound its way through the courts, a letter arrived advising me that in its infinite wisdom, the Court of Appeal in New York had upheld the notion that I was indeed Mongolian.

Shortly afterward, I received an inquiry from the State Department asking if I was still interested in being interviewed for an entry-level Foreign Service position. By this time, I was working as a traffic commissioner for the Municipal Court. I replied that I did not want to reduce my income and could only consider a mid-level appointment. I figured this would let them off the hook, since the court had not said they had to offer me a consular post but only allow me to step onto the bottom rung of the ladder. Little did I know. Back came a letter saying that if I passed the oral examination, the Foreign Service would allow me in at mid-level entry.

I had obtained a divorce and remarried while the case against the State Department went up on appeal. My new husband and I had a serious discussion about our future and decided that if the Foreign Service accepted me, I should follow my dream. He could retire and we would go wherever they sent me, be it to visit the land of my Mongolian ancestors, or his, in Lithuania.

When I showed up wearing a fuchsia Mandarin-collared silk blouse from Chinatown, there was not even a hint of a smile on the faces of the interviewers in Washington. There wasn't much more I could do to alter my appearance to look Mongolian. All day long, as a panel of people threw questions at me and posed hypothetical problems for me to solve, I kept waiting for some clue to their awareness of my bizarre claim to minority status. None came.

After I learned that I had passed the oral exam, it occurred to me that it would be up to God to punish me for my transgression and that we — my Jewish husband and I — would probably get posted to Syria or Iraq or some other garden spot of the Middle East, as proper retribution.

Vengeance came from an unexpected quarter when we were within a couple weeks of leaving for Washington to get our first assignment. My husband had a heart attack, preventing us from going and ending my aspirations of working for the Foreign Service. Now that I think of it, we probably should have demanded a personal cardiologist to travel with us to Outer Mongolia under the Americans With Disabilities Act.

It's not easy being an agnostic. At times it seems as if there is a fine hand at work in my life. Another ten years have passed and, in the end, the mountain has come to Mohammed.

Today, when I wheeled my bike out of the garage of my Richmond District home in San Francisco, my Chinese neighbors were strolling toward Golden Gate Park. Mr. Sing walked several paces ahead of Mrs. Sing, as he does every morning. They paused when they saw me, and we exchanged "good mornings" and smiles. They continued on, properly spaced, faces resuming solemn expressions. I have never seen them converse during these walks. I noticed though, as they rounded the corner onto Fulton Street, that Mrs. Sing was talking on a cell phone.

I strapped on my bicycle helmet just as another neighbor, Alice Wong, backed her BMW out of the garage next door. She and her sister, Heather, own and live in separate flats to the south of our house. Alice, an up-and-coming young architect, rolled down the window on the driver's side and said, "Be nice to all the little lawbreakers today, Aggie." She gave me a mischievous grin and drove off.

Across the street, the Tongs were loading their twins, Mae Ling and Tawan, into their SUV, for their daily trip to daycare.

It occurred to me, as I hopped on my bike, that my Mongolian relatives now surround me and that I have, in fact, become a minority in my neighborhood.

IS THE GRASS GREENER?

Every time I walk into the Palace Hotel in San Francisco, my stomach does a 360 degree turn, reminding me that it is the hotel where I took the bar exam in 1975. Law students who had opted to type their answers to the test were assigned to the Gold Ballroom to undergo the three-day torture.

I remember the peculiar people being tested along with me. One sat across the table and unpacked three containers of correction fluid, six erasers, chewing gum, and, so help me God, a bag of baby carrots, from a briefcase. Those of us sharing the table were driven to distraction that morning, awaiting the next crunch as he chomped his way through the day. We couldn't take the time to alert a monitor until the break at lunchtime. The miscreant was moved to the other end of the ballroom before we had a chance to murder him. He was replaced by a woman who had recently given up smoking. She pulled a pacifier out of her purse and sucked on it all afternoon. Smack, smack!

All this came flooding back to me a few years ago when my son Roy asked me to go with him to the University of California School of Dentistry for his State Board Examination. He needed me to make sure that the patients he planned to work on showed up on time and didn't skip out on him while he was working on someone else.

The new dentists, anxiety etched in their faces, paced around while waiting for the time when they could take their first patient into an adjoining room, to pass the initial hurdle. Patients had to be checked first to rule out health problems and review allergies.

Roy had opted not to work on family or friends. He lined up his patients from those he had met at the dental school clinic.

We left home at 6 a.m. that morning, heading for the motel where my son had lodged Nadja, his first patient, overnight. Thus, she wouldn't have to reach UCSF from her home in the East Bay by the 7 a.m. starting time for the State Boards. Roy told me that Nadja hadn't checked into the motel until 10:30 the night before. He had sweated blood trying to reach her, afraid that she was pulling a no-show. Nadja was standing in the driveway of the motel, smiling, when we arrived. She's a Bangladeshi pediatrician, now working as a social worker in an AIDS program in Pleasanton. She hasn't passed the necessary U.S. exams to practice medicine.

Roy had taken me to the Mission District on a dry run the evening before his tests, to meet Claudia. She was to be his 10 a.m. patient and he wanted her to know I would be driving her to the exam site. I managed a "mucho gusto" in addition to my "buenos días, señora," thus exhausting most of my Spanish.

Sunday, I picked up Claudia at 9 a.m., allowing plenty of time to drive to the clinic and hunt up parking before her appointment at 10. I rang the bell to apartment five, and in a few minutes Claudia appeared, a little girl clinging to her jacket. Best I could make out from her Spanish was that her neighbor, who had agreed to babysit, wasn't back from church, and the little girl didn't want to stay with her father. I tried "no niña," but Claudia gave me another bit of rapid-fire Spanish, shrugged her shoulders and smiled.

I decided to take them both to UCSF. Claudia had to be there on time. I would deal with the child later. I realized that I was having sympathy pains for my son. I hadn't felt this particular kind of queasiness since my bar exam, 25 years ago.

When we arrived at the dental clinic, Claudia took the one remaining seat in the waiting room, daughter Brenda on her lap. A pretty young woman sitting two seats away started a conversation with Claudia in Spanish. Again there was that queasy feeling in my stomach. Roy had told me to watch Claudia every minute, since the exam-taking dentists have been known to bribe and steal each other's patients when one of theirs pulled a no-show. Was that gal there to steal Roy's patient? Claudia grinned broadly. Was she being offered more money?

The young woman introduced herself to me as Elizabeth and, in perfect English, explained that she was a social worker from the Head Start school where Claudia's little girl, Brenda, was a student. Elizabeth was at UCSF, acting as interpreter for another Head Start mom, who was a patient for one of the other would-be dentists. Elizabeth informed me that she would be willing to take Brenda home and babysit when she finished helping the other woman, if I gave her and the child a ride. God must have been on our side! No screaming kid, no fractured Spanish. I could take Elizabeth and Brenda home as soon as Claudia was in the chair.

Roy, accompanied by Nadja, his first patient of the day, emerged from the elevator that descended from the examining rooms. I noted perspiration marks on the armpits of his lab coat. Could my unflappable son have been nervous?

Roy told me not to let Nadja go home, or to let her out of my sight, even if she had to go to the bathroom, in case Claudia didn't clear inspection, and he needed to do the next procedure on Nadja instead. After an eternity, Roy's assistant, Jackie, came out of the elevator to tell me that it was OK to let Nadja go home, since Claudia had been cleared for treatment. It was time to taxi little Brenda, and Elizabeth, the Head Start teacher, back to the Mission District.

By 2 p.m., I had returned to the hospital to hold Claudia hostage until Emilio, the next patient, was cleared. Roy seemed a bit more relaxed than he had been in the morning. Claudia's procedure had gone very well.

I ferried Claudia back home, making limited small talk on the way. We exchanged heartfelt "gracias" and "adiós." I drove home to pick up my husband. Roy had said he wanted to eat out somewhere after the test.

My husband and I arrived at UCSF at 5 p.m., in case Roy finished early. This time, the people in the waiting area seemed to be parents, spouses or significant others, picking up the exam-takers. The patients had all disappeared. Agonizingly slowly, the new dentists emerged one by one, dragging luggage carts loaded with $5,000 worth of the tools of their trade — X-rays, numerous instruments, impressions, vials of various kinds. I noticed that some of them appeared to be unfazed by their day-long ordeal. The Vietnamese reminded me of Japanese tourists deboarding the overnight flight from Tokyo: neatly pressed shirts, not a hair out of place. How do they do it? The Caucasians, almost without exception, exited looking disheveled and worn.

There was no sign of Roy. My stomach churned some more.

At last, I recognized Roy's packing boxes being pushed by an as-yet-unseen hand out of the elevator, before he came into view. He appeared worn out from the day's ordeal. We made eye contact across the waiting room, and I read uncertainty written on his face.

The six-week wait for the exam results began.

Five years have flown by since Roy passed that exam. On a recent visit to the Palace Hotel, the scene of my long-ago torture, I wondered whether at times Roy wishes he had become a lawyer. Funny thing is, after all the effort it took to become a lawyer, so many — after practicing for a few years — long for a different career.

Disgruntled lawyers, are you sure you want to become dentists?

TOURISTS: YOU'VE GOT TO LOVE 'EM!

Like lemmings from the sea, visitors reappear on San Francisco's streets and bridges on their way to our tourist meccas every summer. They wrestle valiantly with our parking and driving regulations. I'm pleased to note that our crosswalks near schools and busy intersections are festooned with bright yellow hash marks, needing no explanation.

During my days presiding in traffic court, one of my favorite questions came from a British tourist who earned Brownie points for addressing me as "M'Lady." She informed me that she had been driving in San Francisco for four days and would very much like to know what the sign "PED XING" signified. Our abbreviations were a total mystery to her.

* * *

Then there was the Texan who felt compelled to break up a fight between two hippies on the tour boat to Alcatraz Island. His attempt had resulted in a broken watch and a scar after one of the guys' earrings had ripped into his face. On returning to Fisherman's Wharf, the Texan and his wife decided to console themselves with a visit to Ghirardelli Square.

"The rain began to pour and my wife and I became hostages in the Chocolate Factory. I immediately consumed enough malted milks and sundaes to require a permanent change in clothing size and future eating habits." He showed me receipts for $500 worth of chocolates he had shipped back home to Texas and wanted to know if I thought he had contributed enough to San Francisco's economy without paying the overtime parking ticket.

I'm well aware that one shouldn't attribute stereotypical characteristics to individuals from abroad or from far-flung regions of our own country. However, my experience with foreigners was that they were unfailingly polite. At the same time, some Americans — and Texans in particular — never failed to mention how many dollars they had spent on their visit to San Francisco.

* * *

People from smaller California cities often projected an inferiority complex.

"Well, I'm stupid and from Stockton, so that's two strikes against me," was one of the more memorable lines from a vacationer protesting a ticket issued for parking in what actually turned out to be an improperly marked tow-away zone.

"I thought it was strange, but we were in San Francisco — a strange place to me, after all," he concluded.

* * *

A visitor from Michigan once made me an interesting offer. He had amassed several citations for parking in a residential permit area — each one worth $20 — while spending a few days with a local friend. His 17-year-old son, in cross-country training for his high school running team, had bolted up and down 124 of the towering Lyon Street steps, 12 times a day, losing 15 pounds in the process. The Michigander was thinking of charging the city for the loss of 15 pounds. "Pounds for dollars," he called his proposition and stated that he owed the city $5 of his $25 fine, but not a penny more.

*   *   *

"May the Parking God's blessings of deep insight and heroic empathy befall the reader of this letter. Amen."

How could I resist such an opening line?

"Please excuse me the mistakes during my vacations with a rented car. I was for the first time in San Francisco. MY MONEY IS EMPTY, therefore I want to please you to wait for my check so soon as possible, when I'm back in Germany."

I hope we all treat the tourists with deep insight and heroic empathy as they converge upon us once again!

"Most Honored Sire: It took me
only two minutes to drop my
baby daughter at the shitter ..."

(My dad always wanted a son.)

CONFESSIONS OF A COURT COMMISSIONER

Under my robe I sometimes wore a tie-dyed T-shirt made for me by my home-steading daughter in Alaska. Only a demure white lace collar showed on the outside. So now you know. I feel better already. But wait, there's more.

Having been raised in a convent school, I suffer from an overactive conscience. Superimposed on that, I carry a heavy dose of judicial ethics dished out at Judges' College. During my tenure as a court commissioner, I worried about accepting a piece of gum from a co-worker, let alone the boxes of candy or bottles of wine proffered by lawyers at Christmastime.

It will ease my soul, therefore, to confess that on two occasions I succumbed, accepting gifts from litigants who appeared before me. So, turn on the thumb-screws, unleash the Commission on Judicial Performance, or better yet, you be the judge.

Both incidents relate to my tenure in traffic court.

One rainy morning, a youthful bicycle messenger named Tony came before me to protest a ticket he had received for making a right turn on a red light without stopping. He had a canvas bag slung over his shoulder, haphazardly covered in plastic, bulging with envelopes and files. His splattered jeans spoke of recent battles with the elements and traffic. His bedraggled blond hair dripped into his eyes. He held his bicycle helmet tucked under his arm.

"I was riding on Market Street toward the Ferry Building," be began, "with a car right on my bumper, itching to get past me. I saw the cop sitting on his motorcycle at Fourth Street, facing Twin Peaks. I'm not crazy, Judge," he continued, "I knew I should stop, but this Beemer was breathing down my neck, trying to make the light, so I turned onto Fourth Street just as the light changed to red, to get out of his way. It's the honest-to-God truth, Judge.

"The cop whipped a U, cutting off a bunch of traffic, and came roaring after me instead of goin' after the tailgater who ran the red light."

I let Tony off. His story had a ring of truth to it.

Tony had not expected to be believed. He looked quite stunned as he muttered his thanks and left. He showed up late that afternoon, pushing open the courtroom door with his hip, his arms loaded with long-stemmed blue irises. Before the bailiff could stand up to intervene, Tony marched up to the podium, and in the midst of ongoing testimony, dumped the load of flowers on the desk in front of me.

"No one ever believed me before," he explained, and walked out of the courtroom.

It's common knowledge at the Hall of Justice that near closing time, the nearby flower market sells huge bunches of cut flowers for two dollars, but it's the thought that counts.

Should I have sent the bailiff chasing after Tony to give the flowers back? For a second, I pictured him on foot, carrying the armload of flowers, chasing the biker down Bryant Street, and thought better of it. Instead, I stuck irises in vases all over the courtroom. My staff and I smiled for days remembering from whence they came.

Another morning an old man named Harold Bunter, whom I've come to think of as the little man from Belize, waited his turn to tell his tale. Anxiety was chiseled on his face.

As so often happened in traffic court, he began by giving me some irrelevant facts.

"The wife and I come from Belize," he said, looking over his shoulder to exchange glances with the elderly lady sitting on the edge of her seat in the second row, anxiously watching him. Both were dressed in their Sunday best, he in a baggy suit, and she in a navy print frock.

"We bought our first car just two weeks ago." His voice swelled with pride. "There ain't many in our village in Belize," he smiled at the recollection. He then went on to relate that they lived in Hunters Point, where the police post tow-away signs whenever there is a ballgame at nearby Candlestick Park.

"I seen the tow truck hookin' up the car, Judge, but plum forgot I owned it. Never had a car before, you see." He looked embarrassed as he continued to explain. "I went runnin' out just as they hauled it away."

Mr. Bunter lowered his eyes along with his voice.

"I'm on a fixed income, Judge," he told me. "It cost me $62 already to get my car back. That's a lot of money for the likes of me. I know I done wrong, but I plain forgot." Then his voice became almost inaudible: "I don't have another $20 to pay for the ticket they give me."

When I suspended the fine, he was profusely grateful.

"In Belize," he told me, "no one would have cared."

I thought nothing more about Mr. Bunter until two weeks later, when I saw him come into the courtroom, looking very pleased with himself. Without saying a word, he walked up to the bailiff, handed him a box and left. At recess, the bailiff passed the box on to me. A tag attached simply said, "To Judge A. Hoff, a gift."

In the box I found a lamp made out of an apple juice bottle, painted green with gold trim, very carefully wrapped in used tissue paper. It had a homemade white shade stretched over a cut-up coat hanger. Stenciled on the base were the words, "Thanks, Judge A. Hoff." The card attached to the shade read, "God Bless You Always."

The Rules of Judicial Conduct say to return gifts. How could I possibly return the lamp? Instead, I'm writing this story late at night by its gentle 25-watt glow, and remembering the little man from Belize.

LOOK MA, YOU'RE FLYING

"So, you're going skydiving," Ed says, thrusting a video camera in my face.

"No way, I'm a sixty-year-old grandma," I tell him, and we laugh. Ed is a photographer working for Cloverdale Skydive.

What has brought me to this tiny Cloverdale airport in Northern California? Perhaps it was the sight of a white nylon parachute drifting down over the Valley of the Oaks in rural Hungary, where we lived when I was four. Did that make me wonder what it would feel like to fly?

Or was it the incendiary flares that were dropped over Budapest during World War II and hung over the city like giant candles, illuminating the way for the bombing? I was fascinated by the way they drifted down to earth.

Since coming to the United States, I had often thought about learning to fly, but it always seemed an idea just beyond reach.

I went for a balloon ride once in the Napa Valley, but that proved a disappointment. It was a windless day, and the balloon hung a few hundred feet above the ground. Besides, what I had expected would be a quiet, peaceful, yet exhilarating experience was, instead, accompanied by the roar of the helium burner, the chatter of a half-dozen fellow passengers and no sensation of movement.

Often, while driving past the hang gliders at Fort Funston in San Francisco,

I have wondered what it would feel like to sprout wings. Once, I stopped there to pick up a brochure about tandem gliding, but buried it in a pile on my desk.

When my oldest son Peter came to my retirement party, he was bubbling with excitement after having been skydiving.

"Wow, I'd like to do that too!" I told him.

Peter was incredulous at first. When he realized I meant it, he became excited about taking me along the next time he went.

"I get dibs on your car," was the not unexpected reaction of my youngest son Roy. He gets his sense of humor from me. When he was seven, he involved his siblings in a debate about which of them would get the gold fillings from my teeth when I die. Now that he is a dentist, I expect he'll want to yank out all my gold crowns the first chance he gets. "Nothing personal, Ma," he'll say.

"First they'll show you a video, which starts by telling you that skydiving is inherently dangerous," Peter told me on the way to Cloverdale Airport. "Liability, you know," he continued. "Then they have you sign your life away."

Colin, who runs the skydiving operation, is Australian, slightly built, with an infectious smile. He is friendly but businesslike, making certain that I watch the video. Besides the dire warnings Peter has already told me about, the video gives the basic instruction for tandem skydiving. Colin then hands me a blue jumpsuit, and I realize that this is real.

"You can get your jump filmed, Ma," Peter says as I am paying Colin. "Otherwise, no one will believe you did it."

It's obvious from the reactions of friends, family and instructors that at my age, I'm not supposed to skydive. I sign for the video to record the event for posterity. I feel as I did when, as a child, I tried to fly from the top of a haystack. That long-ago caper gave me a sore tailbone and a fervent conviction that torn sheets were not usable as wings.

Two other customers arrive, and Colin asks if I mind if they go up first. A reprieve, I think, and yield my turn. I want to see them land safely. The two male jumpers are very nervous: They talk and joke non-stop as they suit up and walk toward the plane.

"It takes 10 minutes to reach 13,000 feet," Peter tells me. "You won't be able to see the plane that high up, but you can hear it. Then their parachutes will open at 5,500 feet, and we'll be able to see them drifting down."

He shows me in which direction to look. At first, the divers are specks on the horizon. Then the blue, black and white stripes of one and the red, green and yellow of the second chute appear. Both land safely, the student skydivers sliding in as though reaching third base. They're whooping and hollering, flying high, though now on the ground.

Ed, the photographer-historian of my flight, spreads out a T-shirt on the ground with the words: "Work Sucks, I'm Going Skydiving" printed across the front. He glances at my gray hair and seeks my approval of the language.

"It will make a great opening shot," I tell him, "since I've just retired." Ed grins.

R.J., the instructor who will dive with me, gives me last-minute pointers, and we're off.

The plane looks like something left behind by the Red Baron, rusty and well worn. The pilot, Bob, rotund and jolly, is already seated at the controls when Ed, with video camera attached to his helmet, R.J. and I climb aboard.

Bob points to the fuel gauge at "empty" and says, "It always says that. Don't worry," and lets out a belly laugh.

I pray they fuel this bucket every morning.

The plane shudders a bit on takeoff, but the higher we rise, the grander the view, and the sights absorb my attention. As we approach 13,000 feet, R.J. tells me to kneel near the door and scoots up behind me. He hooks his harness to mine and becomes joined to me as though he were a turtle shell. Ed, with camera attached to his helmet, is crouched in front of me and will jump first. He points toward me, then thumbing at the door, mouths the words, "Have fun." There's a wicked grin on Ed's face.

The pilot reaches over and opens the door. A gust of wind whooshes through the plane and I wonder whether this skydiving business is such a good idea. The rays of the sun catch Ed's camera as he hesitates only a second, then dives out.

"Put your foot on the ledge outside," says R.J.'s voice behind me. "We will rock back and forth two times and, on the count of three, we go," he continues. "One," he leans onto my back and rocks me forward. "Two," we rock back on our heels. "Three," R.J. says and before I know it, he is leaning into my back, guiding me out the door.

As soon as my right shoulder is outside, I feel the air sucking me from the plane. My heartbeat accelerates as the realization of the jump hits me. In a second, we are tumbling tandem through the air, head over heels, once, twice. Following R.J.'s directive in my ear, I arch my back and spread my arms wide.

There is no sense of falling. We are flying as though cushioned by the wind. I feel like a kid at Christmas. Ed is floating through the air, facing us, making thumbs-up motions. I keep grinning at him. I am awestruck by the silence. The plane is gone and there is no sound except the wind, snowcapped Mt. Shasta on the horizon.

R.J. pulls the cord at 5,500 feet. I am yanked upward, as though a high-speed elevator has come to a sudden stop, when our chute opens and arrests our free flight. It is then that I realize we have dropped.

Now we are upright and can change our direction by pulling on two nylon toggles attached to the chute. The Sierra mountains tower in the distance. I can follow the course of the Russian River to the ocean and see Clear Lake and Lake Sonoma. We float downward for five minutes, though it seems longer. Thoughts of life, family and friends waft through my consciousness. I wish they could experience this. The airport is just below us, and I see Peter waiting.

"Let's walk in," R.J. says, referring to the choice between sliding in or landing upright. It's only in the last few seconds that the ground seems to be rushing toward us.

"Flex your knees and take a step," R.J. instructs, as alas, all too soon, we become bipeds once again.

When I arrive home, there is a letter from Portland from my friend Anne. She wants to know if we should sign up for the first manned flight to Mars. I had not told her I was going skydiving. Think I'll give her a call.

Do you suppose the court would forward my pension checks to Mars?

*Sometimes motorists insisted that I go out with a can of
paint and properly designate parking places:*

"Judge:

You go fix it.

This ticket is unjust — for one thing I parked
at the beach in line with everybody else at
the foot of Balboa Street in the parking lot
between north and southbound traffic on the
Great Highway. There was no cross streets
whatsoever and no painted lines, so I don't
see how it could be an intersection if it was a
turnaround.

Just 'cause my truck's a little banged up and
looks like it just came out of the hills doesn't
warrant a ticket — besides — a twenty-five
dollar parking ticket? I've never heard of
twenty-five dollar parking ticket in my life
anywhere in this country. What's the deal?
Please straighten this out. Go paint it. It will
take a burden off my mind — I'm a law-abiding
citizen and this really bothers me.

Thank you."

Home Is …

Much has been made of Theodore Roosevelt's words written in 1919 on what it means to be an American. In a letter to the American Defense Society, Roosevelt proclaimed that there can be no divided allegiance. "Any man who says he is an American, but something else also, isn't an American at all," he wrote. There is only room for one flag, one language, one loyalty.

In effect, this is asking every immigrant to have a brain transplant. Becoming an American is a never-ending process for those of us not lucky enough to have started out our lives in this country by accident of birth. It is asking us to excise from our minds a deep longing for the place of our birth. A longing for what, you may ask?

In my case, it is for the storks returning in spring to rural Hungary, to the exact spot they had left the previous fall; beaks and long legs, nail-polish red with sleek, white-feathered bodies; the males arriving first after flying tens of thousands of kilometers on their annual migration; the rat-a-tat-tat of their beaks knocking against church belfries and village chimneys as they rebuild their nests.

After decades in the United States, this recollection and many other flashes of memory can bring on a deep longing for my homeland, which I can only express as a savage loneliness. It is something I feel when the hills of California turn gold in late spring or the fog rolls in, heralding a gray San Francisco summer, so unlike the verdant summers of my childhood.

Yet, whenever I emerge from the Waldo Tunnel and San Francisco and the Golden Gate Bridge come into view, I feel, down to the marrow in my bones, that I am home.

Can't these images from the byways of my mind live side-by-side?

Though I love my adopted land with all my heart and soul, deep inside me remains a core that will always be Hungarian. I liken this attachment, both to my place of birth and to this country, to that of loving my mother and father. The love for one does not diminish my feelings for the other. Both hold a place deep in my heart.

And some cried out for forgiveness:

"Please excuse this ticket. I was driving a friend to the hospital that had cut her finger off with an electric knife while slicing a roast. I've never been to Moffitt Hospital before, I couldn't find emergency entrance, plus I was driving west, across the street from the hospital entrances. She was screaming so, and the blood was pouring out that I stopped the car to let her out and help her across the street. I was gone about 3 minutes. I came back to move the car into a proper space and found the ticket."

Acknowledgements

I'd like to thank the many people who helped me assemble my stories into this collection. My thanks go to Laura Merlo *for editing my individual tales and to* Judge Lynn Duryee *for her generous and thoughtful Foreword. I also thank the evolving list of writers in my writing group for their creative input. To* A Book in the Hand, *thank you for guiding my manuscript from shaping to publishing. And last, but not least, I thank all the people who streamed through my courtroom and entrusted me with their stories*

Agatha Hoff fled war-torn Hungary during World War II with her family at the age of 10, eventually settling in San Francisco, which she still calls home. She graduated from the Sacred Heart Schools and attended Seattle University on full scholarship and received her law degree from San Francisco Law School.

Early in her legal career, Agatha worked in poverty law where clients often abandoned her for a "real lawyer" (someone they paid). When she became a real lawyer, her personal injury clients termed it "the armpit of the law." When she was appointed a court commissioner, her favorite moniker was a "fascist terrorist cross-dressed in the cloak of justice." When at last a British tourist called her "Your Worship," she thought she'd retire before it went to her head. She celebrated her retirement by going skydiving.

After raising her four children and dispensing justice, Agatha found time to take long bike rides and write a regular column for the San Francisco Bar Association's quarterly magazine, as well as a book about her mother's Holocaust survival story, *Burning Horses: A Hungarian Life Turned Upside Down.*

Her latest book, *Judge* Hoff, Jesus Loves You, but the Rest of Us Think You're an A▪hole!* is a compilation of her "Tales from the Bench" columns for *San Francisco Attorney Magazine.* The title was taken from graffiti left by a disgruntled litigant on the courthouse bathroom wall, much to the amusement of court personnel, litigants and Agatha herself.

A lifelong community volunteer, she has worked with Suicide Prevention, Food Runners, the neonatal nursery at San Francisco General Hospital and the Volunteer Legal Services Program of the San Francisco Bar Association.

Agatha is also an avid long-distance cyclist, averaging 5,000 miles a year in the Bay Area, as well as in many national and international locales. She lives with her husband, Irwin, in close proximity to the Golden Gate Bridge, where she can be seen riding on a regular basis.

Contact Agatha Hoff at agathahoff@gmail.com.

Burning Horses: A Hungarian Life Turned Upside Down

By Agatha Hoff

Sometimes a story is so powerful that it haunts you long after you've finished reading it. That's the way I feel about the memoir *Burning Horses: A Hungarian Life Turned Upside Down*. Author Agatha Hoff assumes the voice of her mother Éva Leopold Badics to tell her moving story.

Éva was born to an aristocratic family in Szekszárd, a small town in southern Hungary, in 1905. Her grandfather was Jewish, but she was raised Catholic. She had an idyllic childhood filled with piano lessons, party dresses and carefree vacations. She met her husband, a graduate student named Jóska Badics, at a dance, and for their wedding in 1926, her parents deeded them a 200-acre farm southwest of Budapest.

The happy couple looked forward to a simple life in the countryside with their two little girls Livia and Agatha. But World War II changed everything. Éva and Jóska's innocent belief that "it could never happen here" is replaced with the grim reality of life in Budapest under Nazi occupation.

The noose begins to tighten around Éva because of her Jewish ancestry, threatening to tear her family apart. No writer of fiction could ever have imagined the ordeals they had to suffer to stay alive, nor could he have created a character as indomitable as Éva. Her experience is simultaneously awe-inspiring and heartbreaking.

This is not just a Holocaust story, but also a story of love and perseverance in the face of man's inhumanity, told in clear but poetic prose by a loving daughter.

—Living2Read blog, posted by Charlotte, August 6, 2010

Praise for Burning Horses

In this powerful imagining of her mother's autobiography, Agatha Hoff explores how the carefree world of pre-World War II Hungary was made to face the most awful realities of Nazi occupation and war.
— Clifford Chanin, president, The Legacy Project

This is a book that will shock us all out of our apathy to the violence which continues to dominate the news, our culture, and our world. This is a must read for all.
— Sister Nancy Morris, RSCJ, president emerita, San Diego College for Women

Agatha Hoff's recreation of her mother's story presents an instructive Holocaust narrative as well as a compelling family story.
— Mimi Gladstein, professor of English, University of Texas at El Paso.

Available on Amazon.com.

A book club kit for *Burning Horses: A Hungarian Life Turned Upside Down* can be downloaded at www.agathahoff.com.

To book Agatha Hoff as a speaker, contact her at agathahoff@gmail.com.

"To err is human, to
forgive divine and
You Are Divine, Judge."

CPSIA information can be obtained at www.ICGtesting.com
Printed in the USA
LVOW101712221012

303960LV00006B/39/P